Healing
the
Hero's
Heart

Healing the Hero's Heart

by Sue Okenyi

ISBN (10-digit): 0-9798157-0-3

ISBN (13-digit): 978-0-9798157-0-6

Prominent Books™
Printed and bound in Canada

In loving memory of my Mother
and
to all my family for their love and support.

Acknowledgments

I have many people to thank for the creation of this book. First of all I need to thank Pelco's CEO Dave McDonald and the other members of Pelco's Executive Staff for their hearts, philosophies and ideals – for being forward thinkers who never forget their fellow man. I want to truly thank them for leading the rest of us in many wonderful efforts that raise the human spirit. Many thanks need to be extended to those in authority over me and my closest co-workers who have put up with and even encouraged my many endeavors – endeavors that at times took me away from my "regular" job responsibilities.

Every person who helped in the California Memorial effort, whether voluntarily or because it was their job, is to be thanked. I guarantee that many of those for whom it was a part of the job would have gladly done it anyway and drawn much from the experience. You all threw your heart and soul into helping make the California Memorial a success. Thank you to the Orangeburg crew for stepping up and helping out on the East Coast in every way possible.

Thanks to all members of the Fresno/Clovis community and surrounding areas who gave their support and love to our New York heroes. You all have played a part in the healing. Thanks to our local law enforcement and fire fighters for what you do on a daily basis and for your friendships and efforts with the California Memorial. Though your names may not all be in this book, your efforts and love are not forgotten.

I want to thank Gloria Hatcher, "The Brownie Lady," for being such a good friend – calling to check on my wellbeing and giving me support. You lifted me up and helped me to keep picking up the phone. Thank you for inspiring me to share my own story of survival with the hurting heroes. For all you were already doing for first responders, prior to 9/11, you are an unsung hero.

To all of you in New York who shared your lives with us – thank you. You are in our hearts and we will never forget. To Tom and Fran, Letitia and Gail – much love.

Thanks of course, to Neil Malone – for his friendship and faith that I could do this and diligence in urging me to do so. Neil, you are truly to be commended for being willing to and wanting to share what you went through. You have changed my life.

Finally, on behalf of Neil Malone, I acknowledge Dr. Kerry Kelly, FDNY Chief Medical Officer. She truly cares about the people for whom she is responsible. Neil is truly grateful for her care towards him.

LIST OF ACKNOWLEDGMENTS

PELCO
Dave McDonald
Tim Glines
Pete DalPezzo
Steve Weaver
Robin Dunn-Ramos
Julie Debenedetto
Kari Lynn Smith
Diana (Mather) Beringer
Neadly Foster
Eric Duffy
Howard Carder
Ami Davis
Michael Herrera
Mark Wada
Jerry Begrin
Dora Linares
Valerie Franco
Joe McDevitt (Orangeburg NY)
Dennis Dodrill (Orangeburg NY)
Walter Bayer (Orangeburg NY)
Mark Fawcett
Jeff Gong

FDNY
Peter Gale
Joseph Cisteri
Stan Aviles
Tom O'Neill
Neil Malone
Vinny Petrucelli
Andy Isolano
Paul Nigro
Nancy Boncimino
Chief Jay Jonas
Chief Steve Zaderiko
Van Don Williams
The Paolillo family
Bob Muccio
The Burns Family
Mrs. Agnello
Maureen Keenan
The Gentlemen of Engine 234 Ldr 123
Roman Ducalo
Harry Gillen
Eileen Gregan
All FDNY

NYPD
The D'Allara Family
The Gerbasi Family
The Leahy Family
The Driscoll Family
Lt Claudio Fernandez
PO Bobby Numssen
All NYPD

PAPD
Chief Anthony Whitaker
Officer Michael Megna

VOLUNTEER FIRE FIGHTERS
Capt Kenny O'Leary
Urho Engels
Tappan and Sloatsburg Fire
    Departments

Gary Suson – Ground Zero
    Photographer
Chief Casey Clark – Fresno Fire
Kent Burkhardt – Clovis Fire
Ike Urbina – California Hwy Patrol
Tom Zinn – Clovis Fire
Kacey Coulter – Fresno Fire Liaison
Ken Mehrman – Fresno Fire Captain
Chuck Tobias – Fresno City Fire
    Battalion Chief
Jerry Dyer – Fresno Police Chief
The complete Fresno and Clovis City
    Fire and Police Departments
All California Agencies
Gloria Hatcher, "The Brownie Lady"
Diane Westlake – friend of Gloria Hatcher
Barry Hasterok – Orange County Fire Authority Engineer
Kirk Wells – Orange County Fire Authority Captain
Monsenior Salman

Lane Fye – Media Director
ABC 30
Warren Armstrong of ABC 30
Jeff Ashlock – A Plus Signs
Ann Sullivan-Whitehurst – Music
    Director
Mayor Alan Autry – Master of
    Ceremonies
Al and Wendy Hernandez – Fresno
Randy Deaver – Singer
Rhonda Grove – Singer
Dan Johnson – Singer

CONTENTS

CHAPTER 1

OUR DAY OF INFAMY

My morning started as usual, the alarm ringing me awake at five a.m. Still bleary-eyed and oblivious to the terror spiraling toward the east coast, I dragged myself out of bed around 5:15 pacific coast time. In 31 minutes, my life – and America – would be forever changed.

* * *

"Babe, come see the news! A plane crashed into the World Trade Center! It looks like something must be wrong with the pilot!" At the sound of my husband's voice, I grabbed my shoes and ran into the family room to see what on earth he was talking about.

I listened in horrified disbelief as a woman's voice trembled over the radio, "Glass is flying! People are hanging out of the windows! People are jumping out of the windows! They are jumping out of the windows!"

"Do you think the pilot had a heart attack? Or maybe the plane had a mechanical failure?" I asked Sam as we watched the scene replay before us. The reporter's commentary failed to give any clear answers. As I watched the flames billow out of the World Trade Center tower, I thought that somehow the plane had veered off course.

Confusion reigned. The reporter stumbled to make sense of it all for viewers. Sam and I remained glued to the TV. Then we watched in shock as a second plane slammed into the other tower. Stunned, we sat in silence, trying to comprehend the horror unfolding before us.

"What's going on?" I gasped. This couldn't possibly be a medical emergency. Or pilot error. Or mechanical failure. "I can't believe this is happening!"

Though I was totally mesmerized by what was going on, I knew I needed to get to work. So I kissed Sam goodbye, hugged the kids, who were just waking up, and drove my seven-minute commute to work. Surprisingly, I made it on time.

I work as a literature clerk for the largest video security manufacturing company in the world, Pelco, based in Clovis, California. When I arrived on the morning of September 11th, I had no idea that my job would uniquely position me to speak – on a daily basis – with many of the survivors of the event I had just witnessed on television.

At my desk, I listened to my radio all day long. I can still remember the chilling voice of one woman who watched people jumping out of the Twin Towers to their deaths. Then I heard that one of the towers had collapsed. *Oh, God, how much worse can this get?* A short time later, the other tower fell. Later in the morning, the news reported that the Pentagon had been hit by a plane. Unthinkable! Who could possibly be behind all of this madness? Just when I thought it couldn't get much worse, the news announced that a plane had crashed in Pennsylvania. What was going on?

"We had just been to New York ten days earlier," explained David McDonald, President and CEO of Pelco. "I planned a very special trip. We did a lot of fun things, including a helicopter ride from Kennedy Airport to the city. And it was not a quick trip to the helipad."

"The pilot flew us all around the local landmarks, including the Statue of Liberty, the Twin Towers, the Chrysler Building, and the Empire State Building. The kids didn't know this was all a part of the plan. The helicopter pilot made it a special aerial adventure tour of Manhattan."

Two days later, the McDonald family enjoyed dinner at the famed Windows on the World restaurant on the top floor of the North Tower of the World Trade Center.

"On the morning of September 11th," Mr. McDonald recalls, "I was getting the kids ready for school just like every other morning. I got up around 6:30 and turned on [the local ABC affiliate] to watch the morning news. Well, of course, they already had the live news coverage on by then, and it wasn't local, so right away I knew something was wrong."

He remembers that reporters were frantically trying to keep up with the story, and it was obvious by then that this was a terrorist attack. Something planned…not an accident.

"I called the kids into the room, not only because it was such an important news story, but because we had just returned from our vacation in New York. This made what was going on even more significant."

Mr. McDonald was in a state of disbelief and struggled with the thought of putting his children on the school bus. "But when it came time, I went ahead and took the kids down to the bus stop. It was like I was on autopilot. This was just all so unbelievable…a terrible tragedy."

Tim Glines, our Vice President of Manufacturing, described how the Pelco cameras that aided in the rescue and recovery efforts at Ground Zero got to the site. "We didn't know it at the time," he said proudly, "but our guys in New York immediately went into our warehouse, grabbed everything they needed – basically stole it – and took it all down to Ground Zero and were putting the stuff up by the next morning. Nobody in California knew anything about it yet or had given permission to take this equipment. It wasn't until about three or four days later when we finally got communications back up and running that we found out what our guys did. I got a kick out of this.

"Most companies would have asked for a P.O. [Purchase Order], and most would have reprimanded their people for taking the stuff without permission. But this is Pelco. The minute we found out about it, we were all clapping and cheering, saying, '*Yes!*' It's one of those things you should just automatically do, and we did it, and nobody was even concerned whether they had to check with upper management. We were very proud of the fact that we just took care of business."

A ringing phone had abruptly awakened Tim Glines, Pelco's Vice President of Manufacturing, from his sleep on September 11th. "Unlike most Californians that morning, I happened to sleep in. My wife was in Chicago traveling on business, and when I picked up the line, she said, 'Tim, turn on the TV....A bomb hit the towers!'

"Well, with our being in New York so many times, I naturally thought maybe a Piper Cub or one of those helicopters had flown into the tower. But when I turned the television on, the news was showing smoke billowing out of maybe the 75th or 85th floor. I immediately knew it wasn't some little tourist aircraft that hit.

"Then came footage of the second plane hitting the other tower. I knew then I had to go into work. When I got there, I mustered my guys and we did a bomb sweep, first thing, to make sure nothing was out of the ordinary. Then I scaled back operations and shut down services."

Tim tried calling New York throughout the day to get hold of the Pelco office in Orangeburg, but he wasn't able to reach anyone. "Not there or in the NYPD TARU (Technical Assistance Response Unit). It was frustrating. I couldn't get ahold of anybody I knew in the NYPD. Switchboards were down, computers were going down, and if you had a cell phone, it didn't do you any good."

Pelco has had a longstanding relationship with members of the various first responder agencies, particularly the TARU unit in New York. As Tim says,

"We've worked with them for a long time now with the NYPD. The Port Authority has also been a customer of ours, as well as the FDNY. We got to know a lot of the guys there, long before 9/11, also because of our trade shows in New York. So, obviously we were very concerned for their safety."

At that point, Tim and his staff pulled out every large screen television they could get their hands on and placed them out on the factory floors. "There was nothing much else we could do. We pretty much watched television for the rest of the day. I just couldn't get away from the screen, not until three or four in the morning."

At home, after work, all I could do was watch the news. My kids' teachers had all delicately tried to explain what was happening. The kids all had questions I couldn't answer. *Were we at war? Who was doing this? Was everyone going to be safe?* Being in California, we were over 3,000 miles away from the tragedy, but with the attacks on the Pentagon and the Pennsylvania plane crash, I and others couldn't help but wonder what else was going to happen. *Who was attacking us? Where are they going to strike next?*

As the days wore on and air travel remained restricted, only military jets were allowed into the skies. Every time I heard a plane overhead, I thought, *Is it friend or foe?* Everyone seemed to pause. Friends, coworkers, and even complete strangers looked at each other with expressions of concern, trying to find support or answers. It was all so eerie.

As I watched the rescue workers on TV, I prayed for them and for possible survivors. The scene at Ground Zero made me think of the 1989 earthquake in San Francisco. A double-decker freeway had collapsed, many were crushed and killed, but two weeks later, a survivor was found! *Couldn't that happen in New York?*

In addition to supplying the video security cameras at Ground Zero, Pelco was called upon by the Salvation Army to assist in another way. The Salvation Army was receiving so many donations for the workers and survivors that they needed additional storage space. So Pelco opened the doors of its Orangeburg, New York office for storage of bottled water, non-perishable food items, work boots, pick-axes, lanterns, face masks – whatever was needed to help in the work at Ground Zero. In Clovis we were collecting donations of money and goods to help in this massive relief effort – doing what many other companies throughout the country were doing – and more. And this was just the beginning.

At that time, I knew very few people on the east coast, but I mourned for them, nevertheless. In a hint of things to come, I heard that one of the heroes killed that day – NYPD Sergeant Michael Curtain – was a relative of one of our international representatives. This tragedy that affected our nation – and the world – had started to become very personal.

CHAPTER 2

A CALL TO ACTION

Mr. McDonald's first idea for a way to show our corporate support to the New York heroes was to produce a special edition of the *Pelco Press*. This is a quarterly magazine-style newsletter for employees, reps, and customers around the world. It generally contains information about the company's new products, news in places Pelco has done installations, and news about personnel: new hires, promotions, birthdays, births and marriages, and special achievements either on the job or off.

The special issue would have none of the above. It would be mostly pictorial. It would contain pictures of the events in New York on 9/11, pictures of the damaged Pentagon, pictures of the field in Pennsylvania where the plane crashed short of its target. In the very center of the edition – as part of the magazine itself – would be a very poignant letter from Dave McDonald.

I work in the Literature Services Department of Pelco. Our department handles the mailings. My job was to make sure that copies of this special publication would be sent to the people and places Mr. McDonald listed, and in the timeframe he wanted.

Dave McDonald had decided that this special edition was not going to be sent to our usual mailing list only. It would go to every firehouse and precinct in New York City! Eventually, we would also send it to the House of Representatives, the Senate, and every governor in the U.S. But those mailings would come later. At the time, an anthrax scare in the nation's capital was troubling the Post Office. Many of the packages we mailed would not be opened.

Two weeks after the decision to produce a special edition of the *Pelco Press* was made, the issue was complete. In the mailings to the firehouses and police precincts of New York, we included a special letter written by Howard Carder, Pelco's Communications Manager. that let them know they were in our thoughts and prayers and welcomed them to request additional copies. My e-mail and phone extension were listed in the back of the book. Once the publication reached the uniformed civil servants of New York, my life would change dramatically.

The response from New York to that edition touched Dave McDonald deeply. He, along with others in executive staff and those in meetings surrounding the special issue, felt that a permanent memorial needed to be created. A parcel of land in front of Pelco's "Building Three" was designated for what would become the California Memorial.

Mr. McDonald met with Steve Weaver, our Vice President of Facilities. Together, they designed the Memorial site. Steve has a background in construction and architecture, so no outside architect was needed.

The Memorial would consist of a stone monument and benches. They would be made of granite. The monument would weigh 15,000 pounds and the benches would each weigh 5,000 pounds. They would be set on a broad, grassy area framed by flowers. The type of flower would depend on the season, but they would provide year-round color: red, white, and blue, no matter what the season.

The focal point of the memorial would be a huge American flag. The flag would be 25 feet by 40 feet. It would be held aloft by a 100-foot-high flagpole. Erecting this flagpole would require special permission from the Federal Aviation Administration because Pelco is quite close to an airport. The flag would fly day and night; the pole would be lit in the dark by large lamps. seen from a great distance, it would be a permanent memorial of the deeds of the 9/11 first responders. It would be a perpetual link between the people of California and heroes on the other side of the country.

CHAPTER 3

TOUGH GUYS AND TEARS

The reactions to the special memorial issue of the *Pelco Press* proved to be greater than anyone could have imagined! As soon as the magazine was in people's hands, our phones went crazy. The number of e-mails we received was overwhelming! When I arrived at work in the morning, messages were waiting and the phone was ringing. The responses were from area codes 718, 212, and 845.

"I'm a New York City fire fighter and I saw your publication at the firehouse...."

"I'm a New York City police officer...."

"I'm a Port Authority police officer. I lost thirty friends that day. Five I worked with closely. Two were lifelong friends. I'm forty-five years old. I watched the towers go up and now I've watched them come back down...."

Men of every rank, of different agencies, called in. Each one had a story to tell. They might have joked a bit, flirted a little, but then told me their story. Often they would cry. It was overwhelming! These tough guys in tough-guy positions were embarrassed to be on the phone with a woman they didn't know, shedding tears. I told each one that people on the west coast were supporting them and our prayers were with them.

Women contacted me, too. One was a civilian who worked in a business very close to the World Trade Center. She said she had been with the crowds that fled the disaster and walked the Brooklyn Bridge that day. "We'll never be the same," she told me, her voice shaking. "We will never be the same."

The volume of phone calls was making it tough, nearly impossible, to maintain the workload in our three-person department. Pelco has a 24-hour turnaround policy on literature requests. To achieve this, we were all working overtime. I stayed two or three hours late nearly every night, and I could barely keep up my regular assignments.

My workload was growing for another reason. Many people who do not normally read the *Pelco Press* had heard about the special publication. People would see the magazine on a neighbor's coffee table or in a doctor's office and call to request copies. A number of Pelco employees wanted them for their friends and relatives, and the company encouraged employees to spread the word about the magazine's availability. It seemed that everyone wanted copies! One business in Connecticut posted a notice by the company water cooler with instructions to call Pelco's 800 number to request copies of the magazine! I think I heard from every employee in that company individually. Those who wrote in expressed their patriotism and their support of Pelco's efforts to encourage the heroes of 9/11. It was very heartwarming to see messages ending with "God Bless America!"

The messages and phone calls continued at a steady pace for weeks, for months. Early in this period, I ran into Mr. McDonald. He asked about the calls from across the country, and I told him how happy I was to take those calls despite the extra demands on my time. I told him I was so glad to have a chance to tell them "thank you." He smiled. The president of our company was pleased that his employee could communicate our gratitude to these brave men. He considered this a good use of company time and resources.

At night, I watched the continuing coverage of the recovery efforts at Ground Zero. As the television screen panned the fire fighters and other rescue personnel, I wondered if any of these were the very ones I was hearing from! My heart was weighted with such heaviness. Was there any way I could help them?

I soon learned that small gestures can help. That discovery came the day FDNY Lt. Robert Baran e-mailed me. I was becoming accustomed to giving special care to each phone call and e-mail I received. I wanted to give as much support and encouragement as possible. It was a little thing I could do. I responded to Lt. Baran, letting him know I'd send as many of the books as he wanted. I closed with a simple, "Thank you."

The lieutenant wrote back quickly with "Hi, Hi" in the subject line. He said that my giving him a personal "thank you" made him proud to be an American. He also phoned Mr. McDonald, letting him know how much the simple appreciation had meant to him.

That call sparked a directive from Mr. McDonald to all of us in the Literature Services Department. He instructed us to make sure we were not just taking down addresses and phone numbers, but also expressing thanks to all the emergency and rescue personnel who contacted us. I e-mailed Dave Smith, our Vice President of Marketing, informing him of the great number of calls and e-mails I had received so far and assuring him that I was not only telling them, "Thank you," but also, "Our prayers are with you."

That human touch of a personal "thank you" sometimes encouraged callers to share some of their pain from that day. A New York police officer was one of the first to respond to a caring voice on the other end of the phone. He had called at the very beginning of my day. From the sound of his voice, I could tell he was young. I could hear children in the background. He was a young father perhaps, or maybe a much older brother. I took down his information and the number of copies he wanted for his precinct. Then I tried to give him some encouragement. "How are things going?" I asked.

"It's terrible!" he blurted. "It's just too much! My best friend was killed that day!"

He tried to talk more and tell me about "that day," but he couldn't speak. He broke down, weeping, and hung up. My heart ached for him.

My days were filled with calls such as this. I would go in to work knowing that as soon as I walked in the door, the phone would be ringing. It would be New York – another fire fighter, another police sergeant. Messages were always waiting. My heart would break with each call and I'd pray, "Lord, help me to in some way give a word of comfort."

Construction on the Memorial site continued. Soon it would be apparent to Mr. McDonald and what would become a special committee referred to as "Combined Command" that a ceremony should be organized to properly dedicate the Memorial. What better way to have such a dedication than to invite some of New York's Bravest and Finest? A letter of invitation was drafted and sent to the New York Fire Department, Police Department and the New York/New Jersey Port Authority. There were high hopes that some would be able to attend. We had no idea at the time how well that hope would be realized.

Planning for the ceremony would be the start of many long hours for my then-manager, Howard Carder. He met often with Mr. McDonald about the event. Howard had the task of writing all the speeches for the upcoming occasion. The employees watched the daily transformation of the grounds where the memorial would be held. Every day, we heard the growing number of uniformed civil servants expected to attend! The response built excitement in us. We were actually going to meet the brave men and women we had heard so much about. An appeal went out for volunteers to help take/make calls for the event. I wanted to help, but I had to decline. After almost two months, my own phone was still so busy. The calls from New York had not stopped.

But I was forced to take a breather. Thanksgiving was approaching, and our family was scheduled to spend the holiday in Wisconsin. Things were so busy at Pelco, I felt guilty taking a vacation. But we had purchased the plane tickets in July, long before a catastrophe on the east coast completely changed my world. And we hadn't spent time with my family on a special holiday in years. I left the mailings, the phones, and the computer for a week.

On my first day back at work after the holiday, I knew that nothing had changed. My phone was still ringing off the hook. I was actually glad because the ringing meant I could still talk with the incredible people of New York. Before 9/11, I often let callers go to voicemail if I was in the middle of something. I had plenty of time to get back to them. Now, however, I couldn't pick up the phone fast enough!

The first Monday after Thanksgiving, I had an e-mail message waiting from a fire fighter from the borough of Queens. His name was Peter Gale. He was the first of what would become many who would stay in contact with me. He would become a dear friend – although, to this day, I have not met him face to face and have no idea what he looks like. He requested copies of the memorial books. After a few back-and-forth e-mails, he offered to send as a gift to Pelco a flag and banner with words that had become the motto of the FDNY. They also serve as the motto of all the rescue agencies of New York: "Never forget. Freedom isn't free."

The items Peter sent were shown to Pelco's executive staff in one of their weekly meetings. They were also shared with the Marketing Department for a time. Along with these precious reminders of that awful day, Peter also sent a CD of pictures he and his friends had taken while working in some of the broken buildings. So I have seen a picture of him, but he did not tell me which among the many he is. Peter's parcel arrived at Pelco on December 7, 2001, the day before the big event.

It was so busy that day. Meetings were being held to discuss the details of the dedication of the Memorial. I reported for my packet of information early, but I had to wait a while to learn what my part would be. I was to be a "wrangler." That meant I would be responsible for someone scheduled to be on the platform. I was so excited to be involved. The event we were memorializing had affected not only those brave people who were coming from across the country; it had impacted me personally. It had completely changed my job!

Our entire company was abuzz with excited anticipation of the arrival of our New York guests. We had 1,150 uniformed police and fire fighters scheduled to attend. The grounds were ready. 403 white chairs were all lined up in rows. Each held a place card with the name of a fallen hero. Pelco had chartered five airplanes to bring our guests from New York. The aircraft were named Hero 1 through Hero 5. The guests were flown nonstop from Newark to the Fresno Air Terminal. Military jets escorted them the entire way. As the day progressed, announcements over the P.A. system reported the progress of their journey:

"They have boarded the first plane."

"They've been held up in Newark"

"The first plane has landed in Fresno!"

"Hero Bus #1 is on its way to Pelco!"

They were finally here! Even the rehearsal that Friday night for the next day's ceremony was exciting. We did a walk-through of taking the guests appearing on the platform from the Green Room (one of our training rooms) through the maze of production and procurement offices to the platform. We practiced taking them from the platform back to the Green Room. The person for whom I was the wrangler was Pelco employee Melanie Donahoe, who was to sing the national anthem. Sometimes I sang the national anthem for Pelco events, but because I had a nagging cough, I was glad it was Melanie who had been given this honor.

The day of the event, the weather was absolutely beautiful. It was sunny and breezy but not windy – a very nice 58 degrees. We knew this must be a welcome change for our New York guests. They were unlikely to have such warmth in early December at home.

In the parking lot near the side driveway, two fire engines stood with their ladders fully extended upward. Between them waved a large American flag. The New York guests were to walk under the flag as they entered the grounds. As I stood on the sidewalk, helping to direct guests to their seats, a very young police officer approached. He was obviously fighting back tears. We talked for a few minutes and I wondered, *Was this the young man who had called in and had to hang up the phone because he could not stop crying?* I could only imagine.

The media were there in full force. Hosting events at Pelco had become common, and members of the media were frequently present. The turnout for this day, however, was exceptional. Every TV station, every radio station, every newspaper was well represented. Our ABC affiliate had agreed to cover the entire event live. A reporter from New York's ABC affiliate, WABC Channel 7, had come also, arriving on the chartered plane with the honorees. Many members of the community showed up, and one arrival provided a brief comic relief to the solemn occasion. Fresno Mayor Alan Autry was Master of Ceremonies. At some point, the New York fire fighters recognized him from his television role in "The Heat of the Night," and they started to chant "Bubba! Bubba! Bubba!"

The ceremony started with a marching band from a local high school, Reedley High. The NYPD Emerald Society Pipes and Drums played soon after. As Melanie Donahoe sang the national anthem, the giant flag that had been created just for the memorial site began to rise up its pole. It was raised by local fire department members, accompanied by one of the fire fighters who had raised the flag at Ground Zero. Once the anthem was finished and the flag was fully up, the Air National Guard flew a formation of F-16s over the crowd. Aside from

Melanie's faltering microphone, everything went perfectly. Melanie handled the situation without skipping a beat. The timing worked very well.

Speakers for the event included local, state, and national dignitaries: Clovis Mayor Jose Flores, California Highway Patrol Chaplain Jim Howarth, California Secretary of State Bill Jones, United States Congressman George Radanovich, USAF Retired General and WWII hero Chuck Yeager, NYPD Deputy Commissioner George Grasso, FPD Chaplain Harry Burney, and of course Pelco CEO David McDonald. Just before the ceremony was to end, a late arrival was ushered to the platform – California Governor Gray Davis.

Fresno Mayor Alan Autry with General Chuck Yeager.

There were high school bands and choirs, NYPD Emerald Society Pipes and Drums, the Marine Color Guard. There were local singers: Ann Whitehurst, who directed the stage; Patti Lynn, a fire fighter's wife; Dan Johnson, who sang a song we will never forget called "The Bravest." California State Assemblyman Mike Briggs played guitar for New York Opera baritone Richard Woods. Randy Deaver sang "God Bless the USA." After local singer Rhonda Grove sang "Wind Beneath My Wings," doves were released. The beloved folk artist Barry McGuire sang "This Land is Your Land."

Barry McGuire

I had to stay close to the Green Room to get Melanie back to the platform for the final number. Everyone who had a part in the program would assemble together at the end. But I did get to stand in the crowd near the platform for part of the ceremony. I was next to Barry McGuire and I commented on his guitar case. It was covered with scratches, stickers, and duct tape. Barry explained, "This is what I look like when I come out of the shower." At that, his wife gave him a stern "shhhhhh." He turned to me and said, "She's always shushing me!" A little later I saw Barry pause to shake the hand of a little boy who happened to be a neighbor of mine. I was happy to tell his mother later that her son shook the hand of a folk artist legend.

Meeting celebrities was not the highlight of the event. The most moving speech for me that day was that of NYPD Deputy Commissioner George Grasso. To honor the memory of one of the fallen officers, Grasso placed a hat on his head bearing the officer's name, John D'Allara. Deputy Commissioner Grasso said, "Not only was this the worst mass murder of our time, but it was also the biggest rescue effort of our time. Twenty-five thousand people were saved. Saved from what our police officers ran into! Saved from what our fire fighters ran into! While everyone else was so scared they were running out of their shoes, our uniformed officers and fire fighters were running in to save them!" I will never forget those words.

The ceremony was nearly over when California Governor Gray Davis arrived. He had been invited to come and speak but had originally declined, citing other obligations. A last-minute change of plans, however, permitted him to come. Mr. McDonald graciously turned the platform over to Governor Davis. He spoke for approximately fifteen minutes. I had not known that he was originally from Brooklyn.

The ceremony came to a close and the heroes from New York either milled around the chairs set aside for their fallen brothers or they swarmed General Chuck Yeager. They took pictures of one another standing by chairs with names of lost friends. They wept. I stayed close to the platform, which was very near the empty chairs. I shook hands with as many of the guests as I could. Then, not six feet away from me, I saw a fire fighter slip to his knees by one of the chairs. He bowed his head in prayer. The moment was captured by one of the photographers and is now one of the most poignant pictures in the memorial book.

I didn't speak with the praying fire fighter that day, but a few months later, he called Pelco, and we have become friends. His name is Van Don Williams. He is from Queens. He is a military vet, a fire fighter, a chaplain, and a member of the FDNY Terrorism Task Force. As of this writing he, like many other fire fighters still in their prime, is retiring. He became one of my very honorable friends in the FDNY.

That night of the ceremony, Mr. McDonald hosted a huge party for the New York guests at his home. He gave them a welcome none of them will ever forget. The "thank you's" poured in for weeks following. The party was open to all employees who worked at the event, but I was not feeling well, so I didn't attend.

Sunday morning, December 9th, the New York heroes headed home. What a whirlwind trip it must have been for them! They showered the local community with phone calls and e-mails of praise over the event. The "letters to the editor" section of the *Fresno Bee* was filled with expressions of support and praise for Pelco and Mr. McDonald. When an occasional letter criticizing Pelco's effort reached the paper, three or four letters arrived the next day condemning the person who had made the unfavorable remarks. In answer to all the letters, the many positive and the few negative, Dave McDonald wrote one simple response. The *Bee* printed it under the heading *Proud of His Town*:

The outpouring of kindness directed toward Pelco and me regarding the California Memorial is much appreciated. However, far too much credit has been given to me and not enough to others. The cost was borne by Pelco. All of the owners contributed proportionately.

The people who really made this happen are on a list a mile long. Before it was over, there was truly a cast of thousands. This entire community spontaneously opened its arms and embraced these true American Heroes as they have never felt before literally. Restaurants, bars and cab drivers wouldn't take their money. Autographs were sought and given in the hundreds. Gifts, special posters and hugs were around every corner. It was amazing.

The avalanche of feedback from New York all refers to how deeply touched they are by this whole great community. The story of what happened here has spread like a wildfire through every NYPD precinct and every New York firehouse. This whole area showed its all-American pride that weekend like never before. For one, I'm proud to say this is my town …

To the "cast of thousands": Thank you for being so wonderful to so many who needed it so much. It was a mission accomplished, and a lot more.

The memorial ceremony had a lasting impact on Dave McDonald's company. Two events that followed soon after were different – better – because of the memorial. The first was the annual "Toys 4 Tots" presentation. It is a community-wide event that Mr. McDonald spearheads. In the days immediately after the 9/11 memorial, Pelco employees contributed 108,486 toys. That number exceeded the Marine's entire local area goal of 100,000. I had not seen Mr. McDonald look happier than he did that day.

The other event took place the weekend after the California Memorial event. This was the annual company Christmas party. Pelco puts on no shabby celebration. It is always a gala event in a huge hotel – free for all employees. We enjoy great food in a beautiful atmosphere. Mr. McDonald addresses the group, recognizing each department. An "Employee of the Year" is honored and the number of toys donated to Toys 4 Tots is announced. This year, there was an addition to the ceremony. We were treated to a video that highlighted the California Memorial and showed clips of New York broadcasts of the event. Mr. McDonald spoke with conviction and pride. He was very inspired by the response to the magazines we had sent out.

"It costs ninety-eight cents to print one of these books," he noted. "Just ninety-eight cents! That ninety-eight cents has done so much!"

At that moment, I was so proud of the company I work for and the leadership of that company.

CHAPTER 4

UNITED THROUGH TRAGEDY

"Hello, my name is Jon. I work for the Deutsche Bank in New York. I lost some friends on 9/11. I have been working with the Red Cross on a volunteer basis to help with recovery efforts."

My morning routine was becoming more and more emotional for me. The e-mails, voicemails, phone calls, and letters were taking me deeper into the suffering of those personally affected by this tragedy.

Jon and I talked for a while the first time he called. We exchanged e-mail addresses and I sent him some of the memorial items. Once he received the items, we e-mailed each other back and forth a bit. Jon had lost a friend and neighbor, a fire fighter he referred to as Scotty. He mailed me some PowerPoint presentations. All contained pictures of that tragic day. Some were set to music and lasted several minutes. I viewed all of them.

Jon wasn't the only person who sent pictures and videos. Others in New York knew that Pelco in California cared about what had happened to them. So they mailed things to our office. Often when something relating to the tragedy came into the office, people would think, *Sue would appreciate this. Give it to Sue.* So I found such items in my interoffice mailbox regularly.

One morning, a particularly touching CD was in my box. I took the CD to my desk and viewed it. It lasted about 15 minutes and was like the PowerPoint presentations that Jon had sent me. Emotions welled up inside me. I could only imagine what it must have been like for those who were there that day, experiencing everything firsthand!

Later in the same day, I took one of the ever-present phone calls from New York. It began like most of the others: "Hi, my name is Marcella Leahy. I'm calling for the memorial books you have. I want to thank your company for all they have done and I was wondering if I could get some of the books."

Then the caller ventured a bit of personal information: "My husband's picture is being held up on one of the pages."

I asked her on which page her husband's picture was. I always tried to make the conversation as personal as I could. I turned to page 15, as she indicated, and saw the image of two police officers. One was holding up a picture of another police officer. Suddenly I realized … the man in the picture was of one of the fallen heroes and his widow was talking to me on the phone! I immediately expressed my condolences. "Oh! I am so sorry!" I said.

We talked a little. She told me about the friend of her husband's who was holding up the picture in our book. She had found out about Pelco through him. She told me of her three sons, whom she was now raising alone.

I told her about the different memorial items we had. We had the cards that had been placed on the chairs during the memorial ceremony, each inscribed with the name of a fallen hero. When someone called in who had lost one of those heroes, I usually asked if the caller had received the place card bearing the name of his or her loved one. If not, I would send not only the card, but also a hero's medal that Pelco had created for the heroes who had come to the event. I made sure I got these items for Marcella. After a short conversation, the phone call ended with my promise, made to so many: "Our thoughts and prayers are with you. If you need anything more, let me know."

That same emotional day, I received another call. It was from a Mrs. Letitia Driscoll, a woman with an accent that seemed to mix New York and Ireland. She explained that a gentleman named Dan D'Allara had told her all about Pelco and the memorial ceremony we had held. She told me what a friend he had become. Dan had attended the event. She told me about her son Stephen, who was one of the fallen NYPD officers. She told me that Dan's twin brother John was another of the fallen NYPD officers. Dan was now caring for John's widow and her three small children. Mrs. Driscoll mentioned Marcella Leahy, with whom I had just spoken. She told me of other grieving NYPD families. None of them had known one another before that fateful day. This tragedy brought them together.

Later on that same day, I heard from Carol D'Allara, John's widow! "I just talked with Letitia Driscoll!" I told her. "She told me about you!"

Carol told me some about Letitia and the friendships that had been built – the support between the families. It was overwhelming to hear from so many all at once who had suffered such tragedy and to know that their concern for one another was helping to soften the pain. It seemed to bring comfort to them to know that they were not alone. Someone else knows their pain.

After Carol's call, which came after tearful conversations with Marcella and Letitia, which followed my viewing of the PowerPoint presentations from the World Trade Center, I found myself needing a little time alone. This happened frequently as the days, weeks, and months passed. I heard from so many who had suffered such great loss; I listened to so many sobs; I shed so many tears. I also found myself waking up in the middle of the night from time to time trying to sort it all out. I was amazed at the position I was in. How many more would I hear from? How can I listen over and over to such pain? What can I say in those fleeting moments on the phone that will help?

Whatever I said must have helped in some small way, for those brief encounters grew into relationships that have continued to this day. Years later, I still correspond with the D'Allaras, the Driscolls, and Marcella Leahy. Dan D'Allara and others like him have become good friends.

Some of the callers would become a part of my life for just a short time. Jon was one of those. Another one was Ira Rosenberg. He had lost his son, who was one of the fire fighters. We did not talk only about the horrors of that day. We shared about family, about daily life. Ira told me he was Jewish and his wife was Catholic and they had raised their son to know both faiths so when he grew up he could make his own choice. Ira's son liked having the two faiths because he could enjoy both Christmas and Hanukkah. And if either faith got him out of school for a holiday, that's the one he would choose for that day. The Rosenbergs missed their son dearly. They were part of a support group. Even with that therapy, talking with a stranger in California – a stranger who truly cared – seemed to help, too.

People knew that we cared because of the memorial ceremony. Nine months after that ceremony, Pete Paolillo, a Florida fire fighter who was a native New Yorker, wrote to us about the importance of our honoring of the fallen heroes:

> *I would like to say thank you for all you have done for the true heroes of this country (The Military, Police and Firemen). The people of Pelco are a shining example of what it means to be an American. Thank you! I would like to request a copy of the Trade Center edition of the Pelco Press as well as the Memorial Tribute CD if there are any left. My good friend was at the tribute that Pelco put on and he can't say enough about what that meant to him.*

After I sent Pete the items he requested, he wrote a second time:

> *Thanks so much. Again, I want to commend Pelco for all that you people have done. You have all been a bright spot, that has shined through a tough time in our country's history. As a fire fighter, I appreciate what you have done for us. It means a lot.*

This tragedy affected people everywhere. And I heard from many of them. The military action in Afghanistan that followed 9/11 was a big concern to many. I heard from concerned military moms who worried about their sons. I heard from people in various military bases across the country. Many veterans called in expressing empathy with fire fighters and police. They shed tears.

I loved seeing flags go up everywhere! Stores had difficulty keeping them stocked. This tragedy served to do one thing the terrorists didn't count on. For a time, it united the American people. It brought out their patriotism. It bound us together, one people united in pain, in compassion, and in national pride.

CHAPTER 5

THE BROWNIE LADY

On January 4, 2002, nearly one month after the California Memorial ceremony, another unique friendship began. It was about two o'clock in the afternoon. I had been away from my desk for a short time and returned to find a voicemail waiting for me: "Hi! My name is Gloria Hatcher. I am known as 'The Brownie Lady.' How I came to have that name is I bake brownies and deliver them to firehouses. I was visiting a Santa Ana station this weekend when one of the guys there showed me a copy of your magazine. I was so taken by the pictures and the letter from the CEO Mr. McDonald. I would like to obtain some copies of this book."

I called her back right away and she told me more of her story. In 1999, her two-year-old grandson had been at the house of a family member. Unbeknownst to his baby-sitter, he had gotten out of the house. In the backyard was an unfenced pool. The babysitter had taken her eyes off the little boy for only a matter of minutes, but in those few minutes he was gone. She had found him in the pool. Fire fighters had come and tried to revive him. After a long while, they had managed to get him breathing again. The child had been taken to the hospital in critical condition. After 12 days, he died. The ordeal had been overwhelming. It was as though the family watched him die twice. The fire fighters who had worked so hard to save him had visited him in the hospital and attended his funeral. Gloria was devastated at the loss of her grandson, but extremely touched by the support of the rescue personnel who had tried to help him.

After about a year of grieving, she had begun to think of all that the fire fighters had done for her grandson. She realized that fire fighters respond to calls such as his quite often. Her heart went out to them, knowing that tragedy is a part of their job. They have to live with pain and heartaches all the time. She wanted to do something to pay them back, to comfort them, to let them know their difficult work was appreciated. What could she do? She could bake brownies.

It started with one plate of brownies at one station. The captain on duty, obviously grateful, said to her, "Now you have to come back two more times!"

"Why?" she asked.

"Because we have two more shifts," he said.

She gave the fire fighters the brownies, told them her story, and her mission began. Just as it quickly expanded from one shift to three, it jumped from one station to five, ten, twenty, and a hundred. She started a campaign for drowning prevention that became part of her presentation as she went from firehouse to firehouse. By the time I met her, she had visited over 500 firehouses. Most were in Orange County, just outside Los Angeles. Some she visits regularly, others she goes to from time to time. If she hears of a drowning or of a small child dying, she finds out which firehouse responded to the call and pays that station a visit as quickly as she can. She also brings brownies whenever she knows of a line-of-duty death or some other traumatic situation.

Gloria Hatcher, "The Brownie Lady," making a presentation at a Fresno firehouse.

One of the fire fighters at a firehouse in Santa Ana showed her a copy of the *Pelco Press* special edition – the book Pelco mailed out with pictures of September 11, 2001. The fire fighter told her about the ceremony we had held. He had attended the California Memorial event. She asked for copies of our book to take with her brownies to the firehouses.

Gloria called me after her first visit to a firehouse with the books. She said the guys pored over the pictures and cried. The books touched them deeply. Gloria has since told me many times, "If Mr. McDonald could only see what this book and his message means to these guys! They look at the pictures and they weep. The guys in these photos are doing the same job they do. Anywhere something like this would have happened, fire fighters would have responded the same way." The events of September 11, 2001, brought fire fighters from all over the world together.

Gloria continued to call from time to time – every couple of weeks – to request more books. The fire fighters "eat them up like candy," she would say.

In addition to baking brownies, Gloria does another special thing for fire fighters. She hand-makes unique greeting cards for all occasions. She sews individual designs on them. When she visits a fire station, she gives each fire fighter a few cards, telling them, "This is not e-mail. There are no words on the cards. You have to do the writing. Use these to show someone that you care."

The firemen love to have Gloria come. She makes the best brownies – cake-like with double the normal amount of walnuts. Her business card reads: "The Brownie Lady aka Gloria Hatcher." Below her address and phone number is the simple sentence "Fire fighters need hugs and brownies, too." She always tells the guys, "See my motto? I mean it about the hugs just as much as the brownies." Then she gives each one a hug and takes pictures with them. To show their appreciation to her, they give her patches and pins. She proudly wears them on a vest everywhere she goes.

Gloria and I became good friends. At first, I was concerned that I might not be able to supply her with the number of books she wanted. We usually print only a limited quantity of any particular issue of the *Pelco Press*. When the Brownie Lady first contacted me, Pelco's memorial efforts had just begun. At that time, no one knew the great impact the California Memorial would have on the community, the New York heroes, or the world. But Mr. McDonald told us to keep printing the books as long as there was a demand for them. To this day, more than four years later, we are still printing them.

Over the months, I told Gloria about the phone calls and e-mails I was receiving from all over, especially from the fire fighters, the police, and others in New York. She became a great help to me emotionally as I was hearing from so many hurting people. She often called or sent a card to let me know she was thinking of me. We talked together about the fire fighters and the difficulties they face. She encouraged me to keep a journal of all I was hearing. "This information needs to be kept!" she suggested. "It will be a good record of this time for your children and your grandchildren. Maybe some day you could write a book!"

Gloria wondered if any of the New York fire fighters would allow her to contact them. "Ask them if they would mind if a little grandmother from California wrote to them," she said to me one day. "I don't think I can send them brownies, but I could write to them."

So I got her in touch with a few of the guys. As Gloria got to know my New York friends, we would talk about them. If we didn't hear from someone for a while, we'd become concerned. Both of us would write to that person. As soon as one of us heard any news about him, we would contact the other.

We both knew that recovering from the effects of 9/11 would take a very long time. Putting one's life back together after the death of one loved one under normal circumstances is difficult, and these guys suffered numerous losses in an atmosphere of war and terror. The rescue workers told us how, digging through the rubble, they would find bits and pieces of people. Maybe a woman's arm and hand, or someone's foot still in the shoe. Sometimes they would try to imagine what the person would have been like. *She must have been petite and delicate. He must have had a medium build.* Many had nightmares. What they were experiencing at Ground Zero was almost more than anyone could stand.

One worker picking through the ruins who called me was Stan Aviles. Stan was working a one-month tour at Ground Zero. He told me how important it was to go there and find the remains of those who had been killed: it gave their families some closure. My heart went out to him. Every day in that month, he would get up at five a.m. to go to the site. The morning after our first phone conversation I woke up at exactly two a.m. My first thought was that it was five o'clock in New York. Stan and others were getting up at that very moment to go back to that tragic place and look for human remains. My heart broke and I prayed for him and the other workers entrusted with this sad but important task.

Such experiences made our continued contact with the workers all the more difficult. How do you end a phone call with someone who will spend the next eight to ten hours digging in a massive pile of ruins for body parts? You *don't* say, "Have a nice day." I closed most conversations with, "Our prayers are with you."

I was hearing from many people from all walks of life who had been affected by this tragedy. Some calls would end in tears. I'd think, *I'm becoming a grief counselor.* The phone calls would really weigh on my heart. "Lord, how do I speak with them?" I would ask. "What do I say?" Mostly, I listened.

The Brownie Lady helped me sort it all out. Just as I listened to the brokenhearted people from New York, she listened to me. She sent me a book on grieving. She encouraged me to keep caring. And she offered a suggestion that would end up as a source of inspiration both for me and for my growing circle of friends.

CHAPTER 6

JUST A SLIGHT IMPERFECTION

It began with a casual conversation. The Brownie Lady was telling me about her grandson who had drowned. She mentioned that he was a "special-needs" child. He had Down Syndrome. The mention of this condition reminded me of my own medical difficulty. I told Gloria that, when I was born, the doctors thought my mental development was going to be severely retarded. They expected me to have little more functioning than a vegetable. My first weeks of life were very tenuous.

That's how it began: two women sharing similar heartaches. But my story had a happy ending, and Gloria was inspired. "Sue," she said, "You need to come to LA! You should come here and talk to my guys! Fire fighters need to hear stories like this. It would be such an encouragement to them with all the awful things they have to deal with."

I felt she was right. I had faced something devastating, just as they had and, with God's help, I had overcome. Perhaps my story would help them. But why go to Los Angeles, I reasoned, when I was in contact with fire fighters from New York every day? Why not tell my story to them?

I thought of all I was hearing from these guys. What they were going through was horrific. As rescue workers, fire fighters and police, they were trained to save lives. While fire fighters and police tell others to run away, to get out of a burning building, they are trained to run in. They are trained to solve problems, save the day, get people out of harm's way. But on 9/11, they could not solve the problem. They could not save everyone. They saw many of their "brothers" perish. They stood on "the pile" in silence, still, listening for signs of life but hearing none. I knew some of these guys agonized over their inability to do more. They viewed the ones who died that day as heroes, but they refused to use that term to describe themselves.

I knew, too, that some of these guys struggled with being alive. Why did they live that day while others died? I feared some might become suicidal. Because of my medical history, I fully understand the emotional trauma of surviving something that many do not. I understand the "whys." My experience could offer hope to those locked in the turmoil of inappropriate guilt and confusion. I decided to write a letter to my New York friends telling them of my medical history and trying to give encouragement.

My early struggles had been recorded once. When I was two, my mother wrote a story about my life. She called it "Just A Slight Imperfection … But." This is what I wrote for the New York living heroes and any other New Yorkers suffering deeply from the tragedy of September 11, 2001:

Sunday, February 17, 2002

My name is Sue Okenyi. I work in the Literature Department at Pelco. I have conversed with many of you in the last several months as you have called in or e-mailed me at Pelco for the "Special Edition" Pelco Presses and the video and CD from the California Memorial. I worked on many of the mailings that were sent out to you. And at the Memorial I was there helping behind the scenes. I also made sure I shook hands with as many of you as I could. In case any of you can remember out of the many hundreds of people you met, I was the tall woman in the brown suit with long brown hair.

I now consider many of you my close personal friends. New York holds a special place in my heart that I never had before. I am totally in love with the New York accent and I will never forget this time or you. I know others agree with me. You have touched our lives in a way that we will never forget.

I have been hearing from many of you and you've been sharing with me your stories of your lives and what happened to you on 9/11 and what has been happening since. I feel very blessed to have been on the other end of the phone or e-mail and be the listening ear. Now I want to share with you a little about my life. I hope the story I am about to tell you will be encouraging to you and brighten your life at this time.

This is a story I normally share with someone given a scary diagnosis such as cancer or some such thing in order to give them hope. But from time to time I feel I should share with others as well. It doesn't really go along with what you people have been going through over there but, hopefully, it will build your faith.

I am a 38-year-old mother of four. I was born in Green Bay, Wisconsin on December 3rd, 1963. When I was born, the doctor and my parents were alarmed to find I had a little something extra. The fingers and toes were there, two feet, two hands, everything accounted for … and then … attached to my head was this sac hanging off the back of my head about the size of a golf ball!

The hospital kept me under close observation and my parents were allowed to look at me only through glass until it would be discovered what this sac meant. My mother referred to the sac as a "flesh ponytail." My newborn picture was taken with care with my head turned to one side and a cloth carefully covering the sac. When I was ten days old, tests had determined that it was only fatty tissue and they removed it. But why had it been there? It would be nine more days before the diagnosis came. During this time, some other horrible symptoms would evolve that would alarm the doctors greatly.

One thing I want to note here is that I was raised in a Catholic household. And as my life began, my family would make sure that I receive as many sacraments as possible very quickly. I was baptized in the hospital at 10 days of age.

I started to become extremely ill. I would scream out in pain, I would suffer massive seizures, I would vomit often, and my head was expanding very rapidly. At one point, my head grew almost 3 inches in about 4 days! So the doctors were able to finally diagnose me. At 19 days of age it was determined that I had a birth defect of the brain called Hydrocephalus. (My family now gave me the sacrament of Confirmation.) The hydrocephalic child is also known as a "water-head" baby. It is called the "water that kills." Hydrocephalus is a condition related to Spinal Bifida. But instead of spinal fluid building up at the base of the spine, it builds up in the brain. We each have certain tubes that carry fluid in and out of the brain at all times. In the child with Hydrocephalus, the tubes that carry the fluid out of the brain are not formed properly or may not be present at all. So fluid goes into the brain but can't escape as it should. The buildup puts tremendous pressure on the brain and the tissues are destroyed. In the small infant, the head expands and, if left untreated, the child's head can become as large as a watermelon. It causes mental retardation and, if not treated … it kills.

Hydrocephalus is considered to be a life-long condition for which there is no known cure. One out of every 500 children is born with this condition – half as many as are born with Muscular Dystrophy or Cerebral Palsy. When I was born, 9 out of 10 Hydrocephalic babies died. Now the chances are better: 6 out of 10 live. But now, as was true back then, the survivors have varying degrees of mental and physical abilities. Many are kept in special-care facilities their entire lives. Many die sometime during childhood.

At 21 days of age I received a shunt. A hole was drilled in my skull to allow a tube to be inserted into my brain while a second tube ran from the shunt, was kept underneath the skin of my neck , was inserted into my jugular vein, and was threaded into my heart. This type of shunt is no longer used because of the heart problems it causes. I went home from the hospital for the first time New Years Day. I was now almost one month old.

The shunt worked well for about one month. Then problems began to arise. My parents were required to pump the shunt a succession of 25 times at 3 different times throughout the day. When I was 2 months old the shunt began to clog. Two weeks later, it could no longer be pumped. The Hydrocephalus was yet active, the vomiting and the seizures started up again and … my head was expanding!

I did not get through the surgery in which they inserted the shunt very well. My heart had stopped at one time. I was now very weak. But when a shunt stops working it needs to be replaced right away. If not, the child usually dies. But the doctors told my parents that I would not survive another surgery. So no surgery was performed. It seemed a death sentence had been passed. The doctors told my parents that I would never be more than a living vegetable and that *my life was going to be very short. They told my parents I needed special care and that I should be placed in a facility where the staff knew how to care for my special needs.*

At three months of age, I was admitted into the Wisconsin Training Colony for the Mentally Disabled in Madison, Wisconsin. The Hydrocephalus was still active. My parents felt like they were taking me there to die.

As I said before, my family was Catholic, so at this point in my life I received Last Rites. My mother started shopping around for my burial plot. Churches were notified across the U.S. to pray for me. Then my mother told me that out of desperation she got on her knees one day and said, "Jesus, whatever You plan to do, please do it quickly. If You are going to heal her, please heal her now. But if You are going to take her life, take it now. Please prolong this no longer."

No one knows how or when it happened, but somehow during my 3 months at Central Colony, the Hydrocephalus stopped! At six months of age, I was sent home for an extended visit and never went back. The doctors were unable to explain why I was doing fine.

All in all, I nearly lost my life three times. The doctors told my parents at this point that I was still very weak. I had been through too much. They told my parents not to expect me to live more than a couple years. They also felt I would be extremely mentally retarded due to the amount of damage done to my brain. But by the time I was two I was slowly catching up to other kids my age in development.

I did have one more surgery. At 15 months of age, I woke up one morning and I couldn't stand up. My mother noticed that my legs had turned blue. A trip to the doctor revealed that the non-working shunt was interfering with my circulation, so it was removed.

I have never needed another surgery or any other type of treatment due to the Hydrocephalus. I grew up doing normal things at the normal times, always going to regular schools and enjoying life – under the watchful eyes of my parents and the State Department of Health. I still have a slightly oversized head with scars – one large horseshoe shaped scar where the shunt was inserted and a 3-inch scar on the upper back portion of my head where the sac was. My head is odd shaped and has a weird dent toward the back – a soft spot that did not fill in as it should. There are no hats that fit my "dome" – not one – not even the Pelco baseball caps. ("Dome" is a word my oldest son uses to describe a "head".)

Being a little kid with a large head made school very tough. There were some very cruel kids who would remind me daily that I had a large head. I was called "Fathead" and "Watermelon Head." But God was merciful and made me very tall. I'm 5'11" and I reached this height in the 8th grade. The names changed from being about my head to being about my height. It's a lot easier to accept a name like "Too Tall Jones" or "Empire State Building." Now no one seems to notice my head anymore. People tell me I look fine.

I have a very large extended family. Growing up, there were always family reunions, weddings, and of course funerals. No matter what the occasion, everyone would come around. At these festivities very often people would come up to me that I didn't know very well or maybe didn't know at all – but they knew who I was. They would talk amongst themselves saying, "There she is. The living miracle."

When I was two years old, the doctors gave my parents one last dark prediction, and this bit of information wasn't told to me until I was already grown up and having children. They told my parents that if I grew up, I should never have kids. In research, I have discovered that the Hydrocephalic survivor has a 50/50 chance of having children that are either Hydrocephalic themselves or have some other disability or birth defect. This explains the pale, frightened look that came over the face of my obstetrician when I told him my medical history. He saw the inch-and-a-half scar I have on my neck and asked me about it. But he never told me anything. I now have four children, three boys – sixteen, fifteen, and nine – and one girl, seven. They are happy, normal kids with absolutely no unusual problems.

I am one of very few who have survived this well and live without a shunt in the U.S. The National Hydrocephalus Foundation only told me about two others that they are aware of. They call me an "Arrested Hydrocephalic." They are unable to believe that I could be totally free though I've had no tests to prove either way. They say my survival in this capacity is a one-in-a-million shot. I allow them to use my name, picture, and story for their fundraising efforts.

If I were born in Switzerland or Holland, I'd not be writing this right now. In those countries, they don't bother to care for the child with Hydrocephalus or Spina Bifida. I'd have been killed at birth. Forget the third-world nations. There isn't the medical care available there. Most survivors, even if they can live long enough to grow up, have many, many problems all their lives. But I have none. I also have never met anyone face to face who has or has had this same condition – no one. I've only talked to one through e-mail and we compared our stories. She lives in Maine.

My reason for sharing this with you is that I feel I've been put in this unique position for such a time as this. To be able to receive your inquiries on my job and to be able to tell you over the phone or e-mail that you people are great. You truly are heroes. I'm grateful for the opportunity to tell you that you are being prayed for. Little did I know when 9/11 happened 3,000 miles away from where I live that I would be talking to so many of you and hopefully I have been a comforting voice. I watched the news helpless that day and for several days to follow, wanting to be able to do something to help.

Having the history I have, I have at times wondered, why am I all right? Why am I not in a wheelchair or bedridden? Why am I not mentally retarded? Why did I survive when so many do not? Seeing people in such conditions as mentioned above reminds me of what God has done for me. I believe the reason is so that I can encourage others facing very difficult times.

Maybe since 9/11 there have been times when you too have wondered how come you were spared. I've written this for you because I want you to be encouraged. God has a special reason for you being where you are and doing what you are doing. He didn't cause 9/11. He doesn't cause pain. The evil in some men's hearts causes pain. God cried with us all that day as He received so many of his beloved home at one time, many before their appointed time. And He cries with you as you continue to take on the task that has been set before you – the cleaning up of the rubble and the horrible things you have to come across.

I am a Christian. I believe Jesus is the one responsible for my healing. I pray that you will find peace and comfort in the Lord and strength as you continue on. I pray healing upon you – heart, soul, and mind. God loves you.
Sue Okenyi

"Blessed are the poor in spirit, for theirs is the kingdom of heaven. Blessed are those who mourn, for they shall be comforted. Blessed are those who hunger and thirst for righteousness, for they shall be filled."

This is the letter I wrote. The first person I sent it to was Peter Gale, the fire fighter from Queens who had sent in the flag and banner. I sent it along with an old *Pelco Press* that contained a picture of me with three of my kids at a Pelco event. In the picture, my second oldest is standing behind me, holding up two fingers behind my head. The second person I sent my letter to was Stan Aviles. They were only the beginning. Many New Yorkers have copies of my story. I was told by one fire captain that he posted it on his firehouse wall. One man put it in a binder and carries it with him.

My letter, meant to encourage someone, has inspired many. A woman whose daughter was a survivor of 9/11 explained why it has helped so many. "What your letter expresses," she said, "is that we are *all* survivors in one way or another." As survivors who have experienced the grace of healing, don't we have an obligation to extend that grace to others?

CHAPTER 7

NEW YORK

The NYPD and FDNY invited Mr. McDonald to be Grand Marshal of New York's 2002 Saint Patrick's Day Parade. Dave accepted with tears in his eyes. He asked if he could bring a few friends with him.

The invitation was extended to all Pelco employees and California law enforcement and fire agencies. People would have to pay their own way, but Pelco chartered a plane for all who wanted to go. After talking with more than 1,000 people personally affected by the attacks of September 11, I felt I had to be a part of this event.

Shortly before the trip, I received a call from Marcella Leahy, one of the New York widows with whom I had a telephone relationship. She asked if I was coming with the group. I told her I was but that I had decided to fly commercial. "I'll just take a cab from the airport to the hotel," I told her.

"Oh, no you won't," she insisted. "I'll make some arrangement for you. I'll try to get you a police escort. If not, I'll pick you up myself." She told me to look for "a short woman with dark, curly hair and wide hips." I wore a Pelco jacket so it would be easy for Marcella to identify me.

The morning of takeoff, I arrived at the airport early. All the media were covering the departure of the chartered plane. Approximately 800 people were on this trip, including ninety Pelco employees or executives. As I was boarding the commercial plane, an older gentleman, noticing the Pelco insignia on my jacket, asked me why I wasn't on the charter. He was a retired doctor I had been hearing from at Pelco! He had contacted me prior to the trip because he was also going to New York and hoped to be a part of some of the events with Pelco.

He was not the only one. It seemed as though everyone knew the name Pelco and connected it with the Memorial ceremony. When people spotted a Pelco logo, they wanted to talk about the ceremony. At least one other person on the commercial flight was part of our group. A policeman named Al Hernandez had taken this plane and put his wife on the charter. Splitting the pair between two planes is how one couple handled the fear of flying, which was still strong among many.

When we reached the Newark airport, I headed toward the luggage pick-up. As I was searching for my bags, I saw a very pretty woman with dark curly hair and not-so-wide hips. Marcella had found me in the crowd. Officer Hernandez also found me and asked how I was getting to the hotel.

Marcella chimed in right way: "You can come with us."

"Wow!" he said. "I was looking for a bus or cab or something, but can't seem to find anything. Thank you!"

Marcella warned us we'd be sitting on the floor of her van with two of her friends. Her vehicle was brand-new and all the seats were not yet installed. We didn't mind! We loved listening to the New York accents of all three friendly ladies. When Al's wife called him from the hotel, he told her, "Honey, right now I'm in a van with four beautiful women!" We laughed that we should walk into the hotel hanging on his arms.

Those on the charter had arrived at the hotel ahead of us. They had been escorted there by the PAPD and NYPD. Fire trucks had parked in front of the hotel and fire fighters were posing for pictures with us! Marcella waited while I checked in, then she and her friends drove me to a pier, where a reception was being held for the California guests. She insisted I use her cell phone to call my husband across the country. I was amazed at her generosity! I had simply talked with her over the phone, yet she picked me up at the airport, chauffeured me on the long drive to the hotel, and now made certain I enjoyed the party in our honor.

And what a party it was! There were plates of food, refrigerators of drinks, and wine on the tables. There was laughter and singing. There were lots of hugs. We watched a short video showing highlights from the December 8th ceremony at Pelco. Several presentations were made to Mr. McDonald. He and Pelco were given many gifts that night. Many are displayed in our museum.

The party gave me a chance to meet some people I knew only by voice or e-mail. One was New York fire fighter Joe Sozio. He had called Pelco to request the memorial books. For some reason he had not received them, and he told me so! I made sure I took care of that as soon as I got back home! I sent the books and some other items to him and called him to make sure he received them.

Then someone called me by name. It was Stan Aviles, the man who first told me of combing through the wreckage of the World Trade Center looking for human remains. We had been corresponding since then. The day before I left on this trip, I had received a package from him. It contained a letter, some tattered WTC security passes, and a piece of glass from the ruins of the WTC. I was so touched! In his letter, he commented on the letter I'd sent him, which included my story.

Here I was, actually meeting one of my heroes! He stands about 5'2" – small to my 5'11", but ten feet tall in my estimation. He was still struggling with the name "hero" being attached to all the members of the NYPD, FDNY, and PAPD. He had said in his letter, "This title doesn't apply to me. Thank you just the same. It applies to the ones who gave their lives that day. They are the real heroes."

I had a wonderful chance to look him in the eye and tell him, "I read what you said and, Stan, you are wrong. It doesn't take dying to be a hero."

After the party and for the next couple days and nights, I explored New York with two very dear friends, Dora Linares and Valerie Franco. Our hotel was in Times Square. I could not believe this place! All the lights and all the people! To actually be on the street I had always seen on TV every New Year's Eve was awesome. Yellow taxis were everywhere and the Broadway theaters were just around the corner. We saw so much: Battery Park, Liberty Island, the Statue of Liberty, and "Phantom of the Opera." We rode the subway, took the ferry, and went on a cruise of Hudson Bay. The long lines were shortened whenever the Pelco group visited an attraction.

People from Pelco were invited on a tour of Ground Zero and the Empire State Building. I, however, wanted instead to visit the fire stations and police precincts of the heroes I was getting to know.

Dora, Valerie, and I went to Firehouse 34, also known as Hell's Kitchen. We were warmly received. We talked with the fire fighters, tried on some of their gear, and took pictures with them. This firehouse, like all the firehouses at this time, had an area that was set up as a shrine with mementos of brothers lost. It also displayed letters the fire fighters had received from school children. I had brought copies of my letter, and I left one for them.

We went next to the 40th precinct in the Bronx. Police lieutenant Joe Dowling had told me his guys would show my friends and me around. He did more than show us around the station. He fitted us with bullet-proof vests and had a couple of officers take us on a ride-along! We drove through Harlem and Queens. We told Lieutenant Dowling that nothing we had heard about New Yorkers was true. Contrary to popular opinion, everyone was delightfully friendly. The lieutenant told us that the tragedy had caused people to change the way they acted. They had become kinder to each other. Like the flags that waved proudly all across the country in the days and weeks after the attack, the attitudes of New Yorkers reflected the good that rose from the ashes of the horror. What people did with malicious intent had resulted in kindness in spite of great pain.

CHAPTER 8

ST. PATRICK'S DAY

March 17, 2002 – today was the big day! Today we would march with the New York Police Department and the Fire Department of New York down Fifth Avenue in the annual St. Patrick's Day parade. This was my first time ever in New York, and I would be marching in one of the biggest events the city hosts. None of us will ever forget that day. Everyone wore something green. The temperature was in the 50s and felt very warm, even though it had been raining off and on.

We gathered at two corners to begin the march – those in one corner were to walk with the NYPD. Those in the other were to be with the FDNY. Basically, the Pelco contingent was between the two rescue worker groups. I have never seen so many police officers in one place. They were everywhere!

Marching in this parade as a Pelco employee was one of the most incredible experiences ever. The crowds were fantastic. Everyone seemed to know who we were and to appreciate that we had done something to show our support of them. They kept shouting to us, "Thank you!" We'd aim our cameras at them and they'd cheer. Every now and then, a Pelco employee would shake hands with some of the onlookers or throw himself/herself at a group to be in a picture with the crowd behind him. It was a wonderful time. One lady who cheered us matched my image of the average New York woman portrayed in the movies and on TV. She was about fifty years old, had obviously dyed red hair, wore lots of make-up, and was chewing gum. She yelled as we passed, "God bless ya, honey!"

I called to her, "God bless you too, ma'am!"

"Thank you, honey!" she shouted back.

One sight touched our hearts greatly. Many, many fire fighters lined the streets to watch, and they were wearing their turnouts (full work gear). On our first night in New York, it had put a lump in our throats to see guys in turnouts coming to the party at the pier, grabbing something to eat, stuffing it in their pockets, and going back to their posts. Our hearts went out to them that night and this day. They were on the job, in the firehouse or at Ground Zero, taking advantage of short breaks to enjoy something done in their honor.

After the parade, the police and fire departments continued the happy mood with St. Patrick's Day parties. But I had something more pressing on my mind. I had yet to see Ground Zero. I wanted to witness the devastation for myself and perhaps offer some encouragement to any workers there. I returned to my hotel, filled a suitcase and a duffel bag with the Pelco memorial books, and headed to the subway station with my friends Dora and Valerie.

To our dismay, the WTC site was closed to the public that day. I spoke with an officer guarding the site. I showed him one of the books and asked where we could leave some that might lift the spirits of people involved in the recovery effort. He pointed to a church across the street. It was being used as a refuge for those working at the site. The church provided food, prayer, and a place the weary workers could nap.

"It's off limits to the public," he said, "but I bet if you show them these books, they'll let you in."

He was right. When we explained who we were, where we were from, and what we had, they gladly accepted our books. They suggested we take some also to a trailer across the street behind a police barricade. We were not prepared for the response we received there.

FDNY Lieutenant Gerry Owens met us with a little hostility. "We heard about the ceremony," he said, referring to Pelco's event that honored the living and dead heroes. "There is a lot of resentment between the guys that didn't go and the guys that did."

"Really?" we asked, a bit surprised.

"Well, yeah!" he continued as though the reason was obvious. "We still have two hundred guys we haven't found. There shouldn't be any memorials or free trips until the last one is found. Three of my guys were lost there. I'm responsible for that."

We did not realize that some people strongly opposed efforts that memorialized events that were not yet closed. There were a lot of things we did not realize. Lieutenant Owens told us about the high rates of suicide and divorce in the FDNY, a phenomenon that occurred only after 9/11. The divorce rate was up 300%, he said.

"Did you see the gentleman sitting on the couch when you came in?" he asked us. "That was Lt. Vigiano. He is here every day, searching for his two sons." One of Lt. Vigiano's sons was a police officer and the other a fire fighter. Later, I would learn that both perished that day, one in each of the towers.

Lt. Owens was somber as he talked about the work going on at Ground Zero. "Why would anyone want to see it?" he asked. "Do you want to see it? Come here and I'll show you. Look out this window."

The three of us stared at what would be our only view of the tragic site. It looked like a landfill or a construction site. People called it the "Pile." We could only look in stunned silence.

On the wall of the trailer was a cartoon-like drawing of fire fighters on the "Pile" at Ground Zero. A battalion chief is saying to a fire fighter, "Go home to your family, son." The fire fighter replies, "This is my family."

That's how it felt in that little trailer. Guys were coming in and out, taking brief breaks and getting instructions about what to do next. All I could do was shake their hands and say sincerely, "God bless you." I was overwhelmed with a deeper understanding of the task they were performing.

Lt. Owens told us that he could not pray the "Our Father," the Lord's Prayer. The prayer talks about forgiveness, but for the lieutenant, forgiveness is too hard. "I can't forgive Bin Laden," he insisted. "Not after what he did."

The events of 9/11 also left Owens with a fear of becoming involved in a close relationship with a woman again. "I don't want to get close," he explained, "because I wouldn't want her to feel my pain. I don't want any woman to feel my pain."

He admitted that he drank a lot. "Way too much," he said, wincing. "I never used to drink like this."

Despite the desolation that had taken place in his own heart and life, Lt. Owens knew that people who were not as deeply affected as he were reaching out to the hurting. He showed us pictures and letters schoolchildren had sent to him and his crews. He told us of other nice things people across the country were doing for them.

Finally, he turned to the books we had brought. Slowly he flipped through the pages that held the pictures of the memorial. "Wow! These are nice pictures," he nearly whispered. "You know who this is? This is … He's a gentleman. He's a real gentleman."

We had him autograph our own personal copies, and we took pictures with him. His demeanor toward us had changed. He seemed to almost enjoy the conversation with us now. "Show that picture to your president," he told us. "Show it to him and tell him what I said about the memorials." We promised we would. I asked him if I could write to him and he willingly wrote down his address for me. As we left the trailer and made our way back to the subway, we had a new perspective on the deep and long-term impact of our national tragedy.

Lieutenant Owens was not the last friend I made on this trip. In a crowded Irish pub, my Pelco logo opened conversation with two brothers, Joseph and Anthony, who were having dinner with their wives. Joseph was a fire fighter, "the most handsome guy in the FDNY," according to Anthony. Joseph had not gone to the memorial in Fresno, but he knew of Pelco. Like so many, he had developed severe breathing problems from his work at Ground Zero. The problems had forced him to take medical leave, so he was working a side job. The company that employed him makes components for the type of equipment Pelco produces. He had been trying to get his company hooked up with Pelco.

Joseph was pleased to learn about the memorial and was interested in the books and videos we had. Since I was the contact person for those items, we exchanged addresses. Over the next months, I would keep regular contact with Joseph and his brother.

Before leaving New York, I wanted to give out the rest of the books I had brought for that purpose. I had seen how they had encouraged people, and I knew there were many more people who needed cheering. I asked at the hotel checkout desk if anyone could use them. The staff there gladly accepted them. They said they would display them in the lobby. Several workers at the hotel had become friends and had given me their information so I could send them articles once I got back to California. Many were from Ghana. We had connected easily as I spoke of my husband, who is from Nigeria.

On the morning of our departure, Marcella drove me to the airport. I told her about the things I had learned from Lt. Gerry Owens. People in law enforcement, the fire department, and the medical field must have special kinds of hearts, I concluded. Marcella told me I had the same kind of giving heart. She said, "You know, when people call you to order a book, you could just take down a name, number, and address. But you do more. You talk with us … and it helps."

That's all I wanted … to do something to help.

CHAPTER 9

THREE NEW FRIENDS

After the Saint Patrick's Day trip, Pelco produced a picture CD and video of the event. The Spring edition of the *Pelco Press* devoted several pages to the trip. All these items generated more mailings, more long days, and more Saturdays at the office. But I couldn't have been happier about my work. The response from New York was exciting. The building of relationships between Pelco and New York was amazing.

It was Tuesday, March 19, just two days after the St. Patrick's Day parade. Shortly after nine a.m., my phone rang.

"Literature Department, this is Sue," I answered.

The voice on the other end had a very thick Brooklyn accent. The caller began like so many others: "Hi, I'm a New York City fire fighter." He identified himself as Neil Malone and said he had been at our December 8th memorial in Fresno. He wanted some copies of the magazines, our videos, and a CD.

I wondered if by some chance we could have met at the parade or some of its festivities. We talked a little about the event. Neil was embarrassed that they had offered us hot dogs and chips but Pelco had treated them to a sumptuous, catered meal at Mr. McDonald's house. I told him we were out there to see them, not to eat. We thought the reception was wonderful and the food was great.

We talked for about thirty minutes. Our conversation went from an order to small talk to the agony of September 11th. Many of my phone calls from New York eventually came to that painful point. Neil had lost forty friends that day. The knowledge of his grief weighed on my heart so heavily. Forty friends! Even though most of the guys who called me suffered the same measure of loss, an aching stabbed my heart every time I heard another story.

Neil had lost his best friend, Michael Bocchino. This fire fighter 3,000 miles away wanted to talk about Bocc (he pronounced his name "Botch"). He remembered when Bocc had gotten a new car, a red Firebird. He was in love with that car! When he left it parked at the firehouse, Neil had dumped water on it! Thinking another guy had done it, Michael was ready to fight. Neil taped oven mitts on the hands of Michael and the guy he suspected. Then Neil acted as an announcer: "In this corner, weighing in at … we have … And in the other corner, weighing in at … we have Michael Bocchino … " Then Neil confessed.

He really enjoyed teasing his best friend. He told me about a time he jumped on Michael, wrapping his arms and legs around him in a giant hug! Michael thrashed around, telling Neil he was crazy. Neil just said, "I love you man!" As all this took place a girl Michael liked turned the corner and came into view. Then he got serious again. "It happened a week before 9/11," he said.

I tried to lighten his mood. I reminded him of the Saint Patrick's Day parade. He had been at the party they had for us at the pier. I told him how we all got a kick out of hearing the New Yorkers say, "How yew doin'?"

"Do you want me to do it for you?" he offered.

"Sure!" I said.

So he repeated the phrase in such an exaggerated way I had to laugh. I could hear him chuckle, too. It was a light moment with one of New York's bravest. I couldn't bring back any of his forty friends or erase the memory of Michael's death. But I could get him to laugh. I could help relieve the hurt if only for a moment.

Before we brought the phone call to an end, Neil gave me his address and his e-mail so I could send him the items he requested.

Immediately after we hung up, I e-mailed him my letter. Not more than five minutes later I received the following reply:

Hey Sue,

This is a Brooklyn greeting: "How YEW Doing?" I just read your letter. It's very touching. We have something in common… You're a miracle baby, and a newspaper here gave me the headline "Subway Miracle Man." I should have been dead a long time ago, but for whatever reason I'm still here!

I later learned that some time earlier, Neil had been electrocuted. At least twice, he had escaped death while others had not. But he did not reveal this in our first conversation. Over time, he would tell me his whole story, as we built an extraordinary friendship. But for now, he was simply reaching out for someone to understand his most immediate pain. My letter told him I understood at least some of it. I said to the Subway Miracle Man, "I'm glad you are alive." I meant it.

The following day, through a similar phone call, another incredible friendship began. Tom O'Neill was a fireman working out of the Staten Island Communications Division on September 11th. Somehow he had missed hearing about the invitation to the California Memorial. When someone showed him one of our books, he decided to order some for himself.

The call I remember was his second. "Ma'am," he began, "I'm just calling to let you know I received the books and other items, and I just wanted to say 'Thank you." But then he continued. "Ma'am, do you have a few minutes? Can I tell you my story?"

Tom told me about being on Staten Island, seeing a plane flying low, and watching smoke rise up from Manhattan. Because communication was broken, he didn't know what had happened until about 11:30. He immediately tried to get to Manhattan, but couldn't.

He went the very next day and for three days afterward to give what assistance he could. On Saturday, September 15th, Tom was at Ground Zero helping to get water to the fires on the "Pile" that seemed to never end. Tom was in the area of the Deutsche Bank which was badly damaged by the attacks. It was a day of gruesome discoveries: a woman's arm was recovered and someone's torso. As the men were working on the pile, at times a whistle would sound meaning that the Deutsche Bank could shift and could collapse. The whistle blew. At first Tom froze. Then he heard a man yell expletives . The man was carried out of the area. Suddenly there was a call to "Get out!" followed by a big explosion. From time to time during the recovery efforts, the fuel tanks of vehicles that were trapped under the pile would erupt, feeding the fires and starting new ones.

When the call came to get out, a police officer near Tom, trying to escape, slipped into a hole. His leg was broken, the bone protruding through his pant leg. Tom helped lift him out. In the process, a piece of metal thrust itself through Tom's boot and into his foot. Tom got out, but this would be his last day working the site.

Tom told me about the flag of 10-10 House. The name "10-10" stands for "Engine 10/Ladder 10." The flag of that firehouse was found dirty, tattered, and full of holes. The guys who found it held it high. Everyone working the site stopped what they were doing and cheered. The torn flag was the symbol of freedom. For a half hour, work was halted as the cheering would not stop. It was the second flag raised by the 10-10. Three fire fighters from the same firehouse had hoisted the flag on September 11th.

The 10-10 House became Tom's station after his injury. He was assigned to clean out lockers at the house. It was his job to pack up the effects of those who did not return. He also worked Fresh Kills, the landfill on Staten Island where all the debris from Ground Zero was taken and sorted through.

This was the first part of Tom's story. Other details would come in subsequent phone calls. "Ma'am," Tom confided, "you're the only one I've told my story to." Like Neil and so many others, Tom needed a listening ear. I could not dig through the rubble, I could not help a fallen comrade, but I could listen.

At the same time I first heard from Neil and Tom, a third friendship was blossoming. A woman from Rockaway Park, New York, started e-mailing me. Her name is Maureen Keenan. She has two sons, one an EMT and one a fire fighter. Both her boys were working on that fateful day. Thankfully, both survived. This friendship would link me with two families – the Keenan family and the Burns family.

Maureen's son Timothy is a fire fighter for Ladder 123 in Brooklyn. His close friend, Patrick Burns, lost his father in the terrorist attacks. Assistant Chief Donald J. Burns was only one month away from retirement. Now Patrick works with Timothy, in the same firehouse where his Dad once served.

The two friends created a shirt in memory of Pat's dad. Maureen sent me two as gifts – one for me and one for my oldest son. She explained about the shirt in this letter:

Dear Sue,

Just a quick line to say Hi! And hopefully make your day – as you have more than once made mine.

Here's the shirt I told you about and a little story about the shirt.

When a fireman dies in the line of duty, his brother firemen design a shirt in his honor. The proceeds go to the fallen fire fighter's family – or where the family directs the money to go. In this shirt's case, the money goes to the "Elsasser Fund" which helps families of fire fighters who die outside the line of duty.

This shirt was designed by my son Tim. On the front, the #343 represents the fire fighters lost on 9-11 (the family requested that as opposed to Chief Burns's badge number). On the sleeve is 5-5-8087 – represents the signal of a 5th alarm at Box 8087, which is the World Trade Center. The cross on the back is the steel cross found in the rubble at the Trade Center. The white helmet is the Chief's helmet.

Hope you guys wear this shirt in only good health.

Your friend,

Maureen

Three new friends, and three completely different stories. A "miracle man" who was not sure he wanted the miracle. A fire fighter whose job was to deal with what was left of those who had perished. A son carrying on in the footsteps of his father. Each had his own wounds. And each was comforted, at least a little, knowing that someone took the time to care.

CHAPTER 10

A WHISPER BETWEEN FRIENDS

April 2, 2002

Sue,

Just to let you know, we buried a Battalion Chief today, a victim of the WTC! We also had an off-duty member pass away yesterday from a heart attack (not an April Fool's joke). And we had a Deputy Chief suffer a mild heart attack while on duty yesterday. I just came from visiting the DC; he seems to be in good spirits!

Talk to you soon.

Neil

I was hearing regularly from several of the friends I had made in New York: the Driscolls, Peter Gale, Tom O'Neill, Maureen Keenan, and Neil Malone. Neil contacted me the most. We shared everyday experiences, patriotic feelings, and jokes. I would receive messages from him at different times throughout the day almost every day. He was on light duty at this time, so he wasn't working much.

He would let me know when bodies were found at Ground Zero. He would tell me who they were. He would write of funerals he attended. Such heavy conversations coming through e-mail seemed like whispers – a hushed conversation. I knew these guys went to funerals daily, and my heart broke for them. It is difficult enough to lose one beloved person to natural causes, but to lose so many friends so quickly and have so many funerals … How do you deal with such grief? Each time Neil e-mailed me about another awful discovery or another funeral, I tried to build him up with caring words, scriptures, and any jokes I could come up with. Every fire fighter and every police officer I spoke with was going through the same thing. I tried to keep this in mind as I responded to them.

Monday, April 8, 2002

Some of the whispers were lighthearted. When I came into work on that day, a message was waiting for me from Neil. He had tried to e-mail me a picture.

He wrote simply, "I thought you might want to see this!" But there was no picture.

I wrote him back, "I hope you are doing well today. Hey, I don't see a picture." After a couple more attempts, he finally was able to send the photo with his daughter's help. It was an aerial picture of Ground Zero, a truly remarkable sight! I teased him about needing his daughter to help him and told him he must be old. I wrote, "Well you know what they say if you can't do something on your computer … ask your kid."

I quickly got a response: "Ha, ha, ha, and ha!" he wrote. "I am illiterate … on the computer too!"

I just had to tease him one more time, "No you're not! You're just old! Just kidding!"

"Sue, you have me laughing!" his message said.

I had accomplished my aim. I simply wanted to brighten the days of people living in such sadness.

Many of Neil's communications reflected that sadness:

April 11, 2002

> *Sue,*
>
> *The bodies recovered yesterday were civilians, however in today's paper (NY Daily News) they gave the names of two fire fighters that were recovered recently. FF Denis Germain, 33, of Ladder Co 2 (my old co) located on East 51st, between 3rd Avenue & Lexington in midtown Manhattan. The other is Mark Whitford (no age or Co#). Three civilians were also identified.*

April 13, 2002

> *Sue,*
>
> *Yesterday (Friday) they had two funerals for fire fighters! One was for James Riches, son of Battalion chief "Jimmy" Riches, who I know. The other is Denis Germain from Ladder Company 2, I wrote to you about. Today they had a funeral for FF Richard Muldowney Jr of Ladder Co. 7.*

Denis Germain, Mark Whitford, James Riches, Richard Muldowney … These were not simply names. They were flesh-and-blood people that had been a part of Neil's life. And seven months after the devastating attacks, their deaths and funerals were keeping the wounds open. My heart went out to Neil and to the families of the victims and the workers of Ground Zero. Sometimes all I could write was, "One day, the funerals will end and bright days will come."

On the west coast, some people did not realize that the recovery efforts were still taking place because the media had turned their coverage to events in Afghanistan. Though forgotten by many, "my guys" were still hurting terribly.

For them, the brotherhood of rescue workers that had made the losses so painful was now helping to ease some of the suffering. They were clinging to one another for comfort and support. I got to see a little of how strong and important that brotherhood is in some of the phone calls I received.

A woman named Jean contacted me to request memorial items for herself and for her dad, Russy. He had been called out of retirement with the FDNY because the department needed more hands. Jean also asked for items for her friend Neil. He is in your book, she told me.

How many Neils worked for FDNY, I wondered. "Which page is he on?" I asked.

She said he was on page 52, holding lots of flags and a placard. Then she added, "Some call him the 'Subway Miracle Man.'"

Excitedly, I turned to page 52. The Neil I was talking with had come to our memorial, so his picture could easily be in our book. When I found the page, I had no doubt that it depicted Neil Malone. The anguished man in the picture was holding a placard bearing the name "Michael Bocchino." Neil's best friend! Jean, the daughter of a fire fighter, was doing what she could to be an encouragement to the brotherhood.

When I e-mailed Neil about the coincidental encounter, he replied, "It's a small world after all! I can't believe it! Eight million people in NYC. You would think no one knows anyone!"

Actually, Neil knew a lot of people. He listed for me the names of a number of people on different pages of our memorial book:

I was looking through the book and, on page 61, Harry Gillen (L131) is signing the little girl's flag. On page 69 is the grandson of late chief of department Donald Burns. I sat across from him and his family and gave them a packet of tissues. The boy's father is a Suffolk County Park Police Officer. On page 54 is a Lieutenant from Ladder 4/Engine 54, located on 8th Avenue & 48th Street in Manhattan …

On and on … these relationships – some casual, some close – were what kept the hope of a brighter future alive.

That hope, however, was often tinged with pain. Mrs. Driscoll called to let me know that NYPD officer John D'Allara's body was found. John was the policeman whose hat was worn by Deputy Commissioner Grasso when he spoke at our memorial ceremony. He was the one whose wife and three children were now being cared for by his twin brother. John's widow, Carol, called too, and I learned that only a leg was recovered.

I was hearing from those who made such discoveries, too. These people, the workers of Ground Zero, relived the horror of September 11th several times every day. With every piece of clothing and every bone they uncovered, they were reminded not just of death, but of the vicious nature of that death. Many had nightmares they could not shake. All lived with profound sorrow.

The memory of the terror was so strong that New York was jittery for a long time. A loud noise, a sudden movement, any commotion could put people into panic mode. Neil's stress was evident more than seven months after 9/11:

April 25, 2002.

Subject: Here we go again?

Sue,

There's been a building explosion in Chelsea area of Manhattan (19th &7th Ave). Happening as I write. 50 people injured, 1 fatally as of now. News is now reporting possible terrorist attack!!!

My heart really went out to him! I wondered, as he must have, *would life ever be normal again?* All I could do was pray the Lord's peace and protection on the people of New York.

CHAPTER 11

CLOSING BUT NOT CLOSURE

The phone rang. "Literature, this is Sue," I answered.

"Hi! This is Gloria. How are you? How is your day?" It was the Brownie Lady. "I was wondering if I could get some more books," she continued. "The guys at the fire stations I visit just eat them up like candy! You should see the look in their eyes when they see the pictures! Mr. McDonald has no idea what he has done for these guys ... how much good he is doing. He'll never know how far these reach."

I had many conversations like this with Gloria Hatcher. She was actively visiting firehouses, taking brownies, her special cards, and now the memorial books. She was trying to be conservative with the books, especially the book with the pictures of the memorial ceremony, because we were not sure how many more we would print. Before those books were produced, no more than 15,000 copies had been printed of any issue of the *Pelco Press*. The first memorial book, however, had over 100,000 copies in print in its first year! We in the Literature Department were being told that the second book would not be in as great demand. But this would turn out to be wrong.

People in New York kept asking for the books. Letitia Driscoll (the mother of a fallen NYPD officer) called often with lists of people to whom she wanted me to send copies of the *Pelco Presses*. Some were NYPD families and some were relatives in Ireland. I think she had me send books to each family in the NYPD affected by the tragedy!

A request for memorial books was generally my first contact with a New York family, but it was often only the beginning. Many kept calling me. Talking with me kept them in touch with people beyond those personally affected by the terrorist attacks. They could not always share with those directly impacted, the ones who had lost loved ones or suffered debilitating effects themselves. Some had difficulty expressing the depth of their grief to those close to them, to those who depended on their strength for their own recovery.

Letitia's conversations with me allowed her and her daughter Gail to keep the memory of her son Stephen alive. Stephen worked for Metro North for a time and was a member of the NYPD Emergency Services Unit. Mrs. Driscoll keeps pictures and write-ups about her son and the other police officers who were killed on 9/11 and sends them to anyone interested in the event. The Driscoll family is one of the fortunate families. Stephen's body was found intact fairly early in the recovery efforts.

Despite the loss of her son, Letitia always sounded bubbly on the phone. She talked often of my letter, and I know it encouraged her. She gave me her daughter's e-mail, and I have kept in contact with both of them.

Many other people seemed to simply need to talk with someone a little distant from their personal heartbreak. Tom O'Neill was one. He called from time to time, revealing details of his story little by little. He said I was the only one he had shared his story with. This was overwhelming to me! I think he meant I was the only one outside his circle of friends and family.

Tom was volunteering time at Fresh Kills. Fresh Kills is a landfill on Staten Island. It had been closed but was reopened to accommodate the recovery efforts. All the debris from Ground Zero was hauled to Fresh Kills, where it was sorted through for personal effects and body parts. Tom sent me pictures of the landfill. He described a rosary found on the rearview mirror of a fire truck. He was trying to find the owner.

I heard about an area set up as a makeshift morgue. I listened as people talked of the temporary road that was paved to allow trucks in to the site for the removal of debris. As the recovery efforts at Ground Zero wound to a close, the road was removed and another area cleared for transport. I heard how difficult the removal of this road was for the recovery workers as it meant the gruesome discovery of more remains. Sometimes, I could only listen ... and cry.

Memorial Day weekend of 2002 was another difficult time. On that Sunday, May 26, HBO aired a program called *In Memoriam*. It was a video diary of the events from September 11, 2001, to May 2002. I knew this would be a tough weekend for the survivors in New York.

Neil spent the holiday with family and friends. He was having a good time until the HBO program came on. As the television camera zoomed in on a scene of rescue workers lining up to bring out the bodies of the victims, someone asked Neil if he had been there. He completely lost his composure.

"I tried to tell them, through the tears," he wrote me. Yes, he had been there. "I was in charge of holding onto a fire fighter's head," he remembered painfully. Others carried the body, but he was responsible for the head, which had been severed from the body. "I had to keep it in my possession!" he said, the tears coming back as he recalled the incident. "This is my brother," he thought, "and I'm going to carry him home."

The tears did not come from a man unaccustomed to violence or heroism. "When I was sixteen years of age," he once wrote, "I witnessed a homicide and with my testimony four perps went to jail! At nineteen, I foiled an armed robbery of a McDonalds; both individuals went up the river! At twenty-two, I helped capture five or six perps in an armed holdup of a woman. At twenty-four, I stopped an armed rape in progress and chased the perp approximately five blocks where he was captured." He made sure I understand that "armed" meant he had come against people with guns. He had had the guns pointed at him several times.

Such acts were so common for Neil that he did not recognize them as heroic. Frequently, while driving an ambulance, he would hear something over his radio and realize that he was nearby. He naturally went to offer his help. He often turned his long flashlight into a formidable weapon, earning him the nickname "Captain Eveready." But none of those calls – facing bullets, wrestling criminals, witnessing a murder – none had made him cry. What brought tears to this battle-hardened fireman was the memory of cradling the head of a brother brutally killed in the line of duty.

Just a few days after the HBO program, another emotional event occurred. On Thursday, May 30th, Ground Zero officially closed. I wrote a general e-mail to all those I knew in New York, trying to encourage them with the knowledge that my thoughts and prayers were with them. I let them know that they were not alone in their pain, but someone three thousand miles away remembered their suffering.

I was especially concerned for those whose lost loved ones had not been found. One thing that had fueled the energy of the workers at Ground Zero was finding someone's remains. This gave the family some measure of closure. The closing of Ground Zero meant the major part of the recovery efforts was over. The debris at Fresh Kills was still being sorted, but for the most part, May 30th marked the end of recovery attempts. The search would be closed, but many people would have no closure.

The day Ground Zero closed, I received a phone call from Lt. Ed Langdon, who had spent a lot of time at Ground Zero. Although he had not attended our December 8th memorial, I had gotten him one of the hero medals we distributed then. He called me to say that he was at the ceremony marking the closing of Ground Zero. He was there in uniform, wearing the medal I had sent him. He told me he saw many guys there also wearing the medals. It had meant a lot to these brave, weary men that someone in California recognized their heroism.

At Pelco, we wanted to not only recognize their deeds, but also preserve the evidence of their sacrifice. During the weekend of the December 8, 2001 memorial, the New York guests had brought pictures of their lost loved ones and prayer cards bearing their names. They had placed those pictures on the monument we had erected. There were so many photos and mementos that the monument was completely covered! We did not want to leave those precious pictures on the monument outdoors, exposed to the elements. In addition to the photos, the guys had brought other items with them, and gifts were coming in for Mr. McDonald and the company in a steady stream. I received many items as well – shirts, patches, pins. The decision was made to transform the lobby of one of our buildings into a museum honoring the 9/11 heroes. There, the pictures would be preserved behind glass and proudly displayed. It took three months, from February through April 2002, to create the museum. When it was finished, it was impressive.

I have had the delightful experience of taking people on tours of the museum. Once I hosted Mr. Egbuziem, the former Nigerian Ambassador to Tanzania. His son is a close friend of my husband, who is Nigerian. When the ambassador and his wife visited California, I told them about my work and the Pelco Memorial. I showed them a video of the event and took them to the museum. Mr. McDonald met with them, Tim Glines brought gifts, and our company hosted a lovely meal. Mr. Egbuziem spoke blessings over Pelco and I am told that Mr. Egbuziem speaks of the visit to this day in Nigeria.

Thus the books, the videos, the monument, the museum – all the ways Pelco has tried to thank and encourage the heroes of 9/11 – have reached beyond California, beyond New York, and even beyond the United States. The pain and devastation of September 2001 rippled across the nation, but the kindness and generosity of December 2001 touched the world.

CHAPTER 12

BROWNIES CAN HEAL

Gloria Hatcher, the Brownie Lady, called me from time to time. She always asked about the fire fighters from New York. Two of them, Stan and Tom, were corresponding with her, but she wondered about the others. Her personal experience with the death of someone she loved gave her a glimpse of how deep their pain must go and how long healing would be in coming. It also made her keenly aware of the fact that all rescuers awake to the possibility of physically and emotionally crippling experiences every day. She could do little to ease the pain of those on the other side of the country, but she could appreciate and encourage the fire fighters and police within the reach of her car and her brownies.

Gloria was using the Pelco memorial book to bring cheer to the fire stations of Southern California. She was so grateful that we made that resource available to her that she looked for an opportunity to return the favor. In the summer of 2002 she found a way. Two men of the Orange County Fire Authority, Captain Kirk Wells and Engineer Barry Hasterok, offered to fly her and her friend Diane Westlake to Fresno to visit Pelco, meet Mr. McDonald and me, and bring her wonderful brownies to the heroes of another city.

These two men knew what a blessing the Brownie Lady was to the Orange County fire fighters. They had helped raise funds so she could afford to make more brownies for more stations. And Barry had a private plane. They were able to arrange a very brief visit. Gloria wanted to get to as many fire stations as she could in what was obviously too little time.

Two seemingly unrelated encounters enabled me to plan a great visit for her. The first was with a woman named Kacey Coulter. She was connected with the Fresno Fire Department and wanted some memorial books. We arranged for me to show her the museum when she came in to pick up the books. She told me in an e-mail that her boyfriend was a fire captain who had gone on the St. Patrick's Day trip. Kacey e-mailed me some of his pictures from the trip.

A couple days later, I was in a grocery store, chatting casually with the lady ringing up my purchases. We had exchanged typical pleasantries for years as regular customers and long-time clerks often do. This day she asked me about my work. I told her about my involvement in the memorial and how I'd gone on the

St. Patrick's Day trip with Pelco and our local fire and police. A gentleman behind me in line spoke up. "I went on that trip!" he said. He was a fire captain.

The man looked vaguely familiar. Had I seen him in New York? I couldn't quite place him. But when I got home and opened my e-mail, I knew who he was. He was in the pictures Kacey had sent. The fire captain was Kacey's boyfriend! My e-mail to her describing the incident was the beginning of a friendship that continues to this day.

A couple weeks later, it would also become the contact I needed to arrange Gloria's visit. I notified Kacey that I had a friend coming to town who would like to go to some firehouses. Kacey immediately set to work scheduling the visits. She learned that there was going to be a graduation of new fire fighters the day after Gloria's arrival. She asked me if I could bring Gloria there. Kacey also learned that the "Hero" postage stamp would be unveiled in two locations when Gloria was to be in town. We would try to make it to one of those.

Kacey and I wanted to raise funds for Gloria as she does everything out of her own pocket. I got permission from Pelco to solicit funds in the company. I wrote a brief bio about the Brownie Lady and circulated it along with photos and envelopes for donations. Kacey did a similar appeal at the firehouses.

All the plans were in place. I scheduled time off from work so I could pick up the Brownie Lady and her friends from the airport and take them around. I would give them a tour of the museum at Pelco, take them to lunch, and shuttle them to three fire stations. They would leave the next day.

A frantic e-mail from Kacey late in the afternoon radically changed our plans. It just said, "The head Fire Chief has sent out a Press Release. Call me immediately!" The fire chief had informed the media of Gloria's coming and scheduled her to visit all the firehouses in Fresno. *All* the firehouses! Now I was frantic, too. The Brownie Lady was bringing 100 brownies with her, enough to cover only three stations.

"Looks like we need to do some baking!" I told Kacey. Kacey had calculated how many fire fighters were at each station. We would need at least 300 more brownies. Kacey generously offered to make some. Vickie Lane, another Pelco employee, overheard my harried tale and said she would bake four dozen. In one night, I baked 140 brownies.

When Gloria arrived, Pelco treated her like the very special person she is. I met the small plane at the airport. I did not know how to recognize the Brownie Lady, but when a small woman with dark hair specked with gray highlights walked down the steps, I knew it was her. She was wearing a blue vest with patches – fire department and police department patches. I greeted Gloria,

Diane, and the two Orange County fire fighters with gift bags from Pelco. Each contained the memorial books, a video, a shirt, and a hat.

The airport was a short drive from Pelco, where a wonderful lunch was waiting for them in the company café. A special table had been set with linen tablecloth and napkins and elegant china. This was treatment reserved for honored guests. Co-owner Tim Glines gave each person in the little party a hero's welcome. Pelco had designed and given a hero's medal to each of the police and fire fighters who had come to the memorial ceremony from New York and each surviving family member in memory of their lost loved one. Tim gave Gloria, Diane, Barry, and Kirk each one of these medals, making Gloria and Diane the only civilians to own one. They had not experienced the horrors of September 11th close-up, but they had reached out to help heal those who had. And they were giving of their time and resources to lend support to people who performed sacrificial deeds every day. That made them heroes.

Tim showed Gloria and her friends around. He took us to the museum that commemorated the people and events of 9/11. Once inside, Tim disappeared up the stairs toward Mr. McDonald's office. To our surprise, Dave McDonald came down and met our guests. He wrapped his arm around Gloria and gave her a very personal guided tour of the museum, stopping to explain each display. He told her she was welcome to as many books as she wanted. "Just call Sue and she'll send them to you," he told her. She thanked him for doing so much good for so many people.

After the tour of the museum, we headed to the first firehouse on our schedule. Kacey met us outside and warned us that the media were inside. Gloria didn't mind the interview. She was happy for people to know of her work. It would remind the public of the difficult and important work our nation's first responders perform. Perhaps it would inspire someone else to do something tangible to encourage their fire fighters and police.

We spent two and a half days going from firehouse to firehouse, delivering brownies and making some very special connections with my own local heroes. Sharing with the guys and having them open up to us was wonderful. At some of the stations, we could sit and talk for some time. At others, a call would come and the guys would have to leave. When things were quiet with no calls, Gloria could really talk with the guys. She shared with them some pictures she always presents to the fire fighters she visits and had them pick out cards she had made for them.

Some of the visits had fun surprises for us. At Station 3, which the men call "The Rock," we attended a gathering for the group graduating from the fire service training. We got to see several different training practices. We watched the new fire fighters climb the outside of a burning building, run through the doors of a building that was on fire and open the windows, and put out the flames of a burning car. Our respect and admiration for these living heroes grew.

At Station 34 in Clovis, we got to see a state-of-the-art firehouse. It does not look anything like a traditional firehouse except for a couple of antique fire engines. Captain Tom Zinn, the Silver Fox, showed us around. He let us climb into one of the old engines.

The firemen at one house gave Gloria and Diane a ride on the fire truck they actually used. They were just going around the block when a call came in. It was a big fire, requiring three engines. The fire engine took off with Gloria and Diane inside. Kacey and I had to jump in a car and follow behind them. "We have to get them out of there!" Kacey exclaimed.

Dinner with fire fighters in a stationhouse was a treat each night. We loved listening to the firemen's stories, and they loved knowing that we truly appreciated what they do. Of course, we left them brownies for dessert.

Gloria had come to pay tribute to the fire fighters, but she found herself being feted. At Station 13, the hero stamp was unveiled. The unveiling ceremony seemed a fitting time and place for a special presentation for the Brownie Lady. The Postmaster gave his permission, so I stood near the easel on which the image of the new stamp was displayed. Standing next to a picture that honored the 9/11 heroes, I honored one of the heroes of the healing process. I explained who Gloria was and what it was she did. I then presented her with the funds we had raised for her work.

Gloria was also honored at City Hall. We went there to attend a graduation of a fire fighters' class. To our surprise, the leaders conducting the ceremony paused to honor Gloria for her efforts in encouraging fire fighters.

We didn't get to all the fire stations, but Gloria returned a month later and we went on another brownie baking rampage and whirlwind tour. Gloria did not do this to receive accolades. She did not do it for all the fun it ended up being. An e-mail from her daughter explains why taking brownies to firemen is so important to Gloria:

> My mom ... tells me that you have touched many people's lives in such a positive way by helping them to process their grief. When I lost my son Brandon I was lucky enough to have one friend that just listened to me and didn't tell me to get over it, or that it was his time, or other rhetoric. She just stood by me and was there for me. I know that not everyone is so lucky and it is wonderful to know that you were able to be there for people you didn't even know. Thank you for that.
>
> Working in the fire service myself, I know how difficult it is when one of our own is lost. People like you and my mother make it easier. ... Every time she goes to

a station she takes the books you gave her and gives them out to the firemen. I can't tell you how many down here know of the work you have done.

Gloria bakes and delivers brownies and good cheer because she and her daughter have suffered great loss and understand what it takes to heal from that loss. She does it because she has been blessed personally by the bravery and compassion of fire fighters. She does it because it is one way to say, "Thank you for doing something so difficult for other people." Gloria has found that brownies can heal.

CHAPTER 13

SOMEONE REMEMBERS YOU
NEIL MALONE'S 9/11 STORY

"I'll cry with you," she whispered. "Until we run out of tears …
Even if it's forever. We'll do it together." There it was …
a simple promise of connection. The loving alliance of
grief and hope that blesses both our breaking apart
and our coming together again.

– Molly Fumia, Safe Passage

It was late July 2002 in the middle of the afternoon. "Linda's Catering" truck was parked near the Shipping Department, as it usually is at that time of day. I decided to grab something from the truck. On the way back, I stopped to chat with Ami Davis, who was sitting at one of the outside tables.

We spoke about the friendships that were forming between Pelco employees in California and people in New York. Ami and her father had gotten to know some of the bagpipers. I mentioned my correspondence with Neil Malone. In my description of him, I mentioned that he had been electrocuted. She knew exactly who I was talking about! At the memorial event in December, she had been in charge of directing our New York guests at the hotel. She had met Neil and his friends at the hotel. She said they had impressed her because the first thing they wanted to do was find a church so they could go to Mass. He had told her his story about the electrocution and had given her a pin.

It intrigued me that Neil had been willing to share some of his story. All I knew was that he had been electrocuted and lost forty of his friends. I knew that no matter what his full story was, it was a painful experience, as was the case for every person involved in the September 11th tragedy. I jotted a quick note to Neil about my conversation with Ami. In the subject line I put, "Someone remembers you." I told him how grateful we at Pelco were for the friendships we had gained with those on his side of the country. I had no idea that this brief e-mail would suddenly open the way for him to share his painful story with me. He wrote me back the same day.

He didn't remember Ami. He did recall talking with a woman of Syrian descent. He explained why his memory was foggy: "You see, I was on medication," he wrote. "I had planned on taking my life! Late Sat. nite I started drinking heavily, which led to the early morning hours of Sun." In those early morning hours, he talked for about two hours with the young Syrian woman. He told her he planned to end his life and she begged him not to. She cried with him. During those two hours, he told her why he had accepted Pelco's invitation to come to California. He wrote the story for me:

It was Aug. 5, 2001. I was working on the ambulance from 1800 hours (6pm) to 0200 hrs. At about 7pm, we came upon an accident scene. All these cars were pulling up to the scene. Triple parking on the avenue, with all different state plates (NY, PENN, CONN.). This 8-year-old Moroccan boy was surrounded by all these adults. After a stand off, we were able to get the child into the bus (ambulance). When the father and uncle left the bus for a few moments, the boy asked me if I work 9-11. I replied, this is a 911 bus. He said no, do you work on 9-11? Again I told him it was a 911 bus. He said no, you don't understand, are you working on 9-11? I said I might be because this was my second job; my first job was a fire fighter! His mouth hit the floor! Twice I tried to get out of him what was going to happen. Both times he looked out the rear window and, on the second time he started to tell me, when his father opened the door and started screaming in Arabic. The boy becomes quiet and the father turns to me with his finger in my face and asks, what were you talking about? In a calm voice I told him to take his finger out of my face! Again he asked me with his finger in my face. I told him to remove it, or we were going to have a problem. With that, he sat down! And I explained, we were talking about my bus. How when you call we come, but we were passing by and stopped. I never mentioned the numbers 911. So on Aug 6, 2001, I went to work at the firehouse and, at approx. 7pm, I was electrocuted and lost my memory until the first week of December. That's when I started having these "nightmares." After two days or so, I realized it wasn't a dream, it was reality!!! Off I went to CA. To ask for forgiveness of my 40 friends that were killed! That Sunday night I drank until about 3 or 4 am, telling this girl of my intentions and her begging me not to do it! I left her in the bar, went to my room, walked around the bed to the radio. I pushed the sleep button, which goes off in 59 minutes. Walked to the other side of bed, grabbed my meds (30 pills), asked for forgiveness again. Next thing I know, I wake up the radio is playing, it's 7am and the song on the radio is "I'll Be Home For Christmas"!!! The pills were all over the bed!

I was overwhelmed by what I read. It gave me a glimpse at how deeply he was still hurting. He had lost forty friends, and that alone would be enough to drown an ordinary man in sorrow. But in addition, he felt responsible for their deaths, as though he should have foreseen and prevented the tragedy. He wished he had died in their place. How could I help him? What do you say to someone who feels such intense guilt for something someone did to him? I wrote:

Dear Neil,

I am sitting here reading this dumbfounded. First of all, I want to thank you for sharing this with me. I cannot tell you what this means to me! This must be extremely hard for you to tell. You have been through an awful lot. This must have been and still be such a heavy burden for you. Dude, my prayers continue for you. There is a reason you are still alive. God wants you alive. I cannot explain why certain of your friends died and certain ones lived or why you were where you were at the time you were. Being the survivor I am, I have looked at people in wheelchairs and people with mental handicaps that the rest of society doesn't want to really look at and have thought, that could have and should have been me! But for whatever reason I'm alive and with, I believe, all my mental faculties working. When my mother first told me, at age 16, certain things like: "You were born with a 10% chance to live," "Once the shunt stopped working they said you had no more chance," "They said you would be nothing more than a living vegetable" – I would pace the floor for hours asking God, "Why?" I could tell you much more but I don't want to talk about me right now. Anyway, I am here and you are here. ... For all you have been through, Neil, I know there is one person who knows all of it and understands it, and his name is Jesus. I will be praying for your peace of mind and strength of spirit. About all I can say is my heart weeps with yours and I will always listen to you and pray for you. Jesus is with you always.

I later understood that when one person's heart weeps with another's, healing is taking place.

CHAPTER 14

ONE YEAR LATER

PRESS RELEASE

For Immediate Release: 11:00 A.M. PDST, August 21, 2002
For Further Information Contact   Tim Glines, Vice President, Pelco
                                                      or
                                                      Janet Stoll, Public Information Officer,
                                                      City of Clovis.

**CALIFORNIA MEMORIAL EVENTS
PLANNED FOR SEPTEMBER 11, 2002**

On September 11, 2002, there will be two commemorative events at the California Memorial in Clovis. Guests of honor will include small contingents of New York City Police Officers, New York City Fire fighters, Port Authority Police Officers, as well as the New York City Police Department Emerald Society Pipes and Drums. At 5:30 A.M. there will be a brief ceremony coinciding with the time of the first attack (5:46 A.M.) against the World Trade Center in New York. This event will include the playing of taps as the Memorial Flag is lowered to half staff by the U.S. Marine Corps, Amazing Grace performed by the NYPD Bagpipe Band, and a twenty-one gun salute.

At 12:00 Noon there will be an approximately one-hour-long program of music and remembrances including performances by several artists from the December 8th Dedication Ceremony; including the NYPD Bagpipe Band. Fresno Mayor Alan Autry will act as Master of Ceremonies. Speakers will include California Secretary of State Bill Jones and Chief Anthony Whitaker of the Port Authority of New York and New Jersey Police Department. Chief Whitaker was one of the World Trade Center Commanding Officers at the time of the initial attack and during rescue and recovery operations. The ceremony will also include a fly-over and release of white doves.

The public is invited to attend both events and show their respect for the 403 fallen heroes from September 11, 2001, as well as for the thousands of surviving heroes who participated in rescue and recovery operations. A special reserved section will be provided for area law enforcement and firefighting personnel. The California Memorial is located on Pelco's corporate campus near Dakota and Peach Avenues. Traffic management and parking plans are being finalized by the cities of Clovis and Fresno and will be announced prior to the event. Live television coverage is not planned. The California Memorial Museum will be open to the public all day, as it is every day except Sunday.

The California Memorial was built following the September 11th, 2001, attacks to honor our fallen heroes and dedicated on December 8th, 2001. The dedication ceremony included 1,150 New York City Police Officers, New York Fire fighters, and Port Authority Police Officers. Subsequently, these New York guests of honor presented Pelco with hundreds of historic memorabilia items relating to the disaster, which are on display in the California Memorial Museum located near the Monument.

END OF PRESS RELEASE

For the first-year anniversary of the terrorist attacks, Pelco was planning an observance ceremony. We were looking for people from New York to attend as we were bringing small contingents from three agencies to participate in the events. I submitted several names for consideration. Neil Malone's was among them.

I let Neil know that I put in his name. I thought it might be good for him to come to California again and leave with a happier memory. I knew the day would be hard on him whatever he did. I was getting increasingly worried about him. His messages were sad and troubling: "We're still burying from 9-11! Last week, they found a 7-inch pelvic bone on one of the rooftops!"

Just knowing how many friends he had lost and how frequently he was attending funerals made my heart sink. How would he and the other rescuers get through this time? What about the other surviving family members? What would the first anniversary of the day that completely devastated their lives be like? I felt that keeping in touch with Neil and others was very important. I wanted them to know that we had not forgotten them. We were still hearing their hurts and supporting them.

Sometimes the hurts showed themselves in emotional complaints. One day a very tearful woman with a heavy accent chided me.

"My name is Rita Agnello," she began. "I want the books from the memorial. My son is pictured on one of the pages of your book."

"Which page?" I asked, trying to let her know I was sorry for her loss.

"It's page sixteen. His name is on the chair. Why you not take a better picture of my son's chair?" she asked. "Others, their name appears better. Why you not take my son's well? My son's name should appear more clearly."

Her anguish was so great that my heart broke for her. To her, there was no one more important than her son Joseph. That's how it was for so many who called. Of the thousands who died, they wanted to know that *one* was noticed, mourned, and remembered. I did what I could to give them that assurance.

I took down Mrs. Agnello's information and promised to send her the memorial books. I usually asked people calling in if they had received the card with the name of their loved one from the chair where we had placed them. If not, I would request one. I would also get them copies of the medal we gave to each hero who came from New York. I made sure Mrs. Agnello received everything.

As the actual anniversary of September 11th approached, I had many phone calls from heroes and survivors. So much about the 9/11 tragedy was being aired, and the reminders were difficult for many who were there that day. Tom O'Neill called every time he watched the news. He would tell me the coverage was too much for him. Tom would clip "Love Letters from 9/11," a section that appeared daily in the Staten Island newspaper. He would send them to me to show me that the disaster was still in the papers every day and the wounds were still raw.

A girlfriend of a fire fighter e-mailed me a lot as the first anniversary neared. She talked about the anxiety that was surfacing in anticipation of the day. She told me of days she would cry, days her boyfriend would weep, and days they both would dissolve in tears. She was suffering from anxiety and shortness of breath. Her boyfriend tried to work around the clock, helping out at the site. He would somehow find time to attend every ceremony and church service held at the location. She was concerned about the amount of time he was spending there. Also she was so concerned for all the "stuff" everyone was breathing in. I prayed a lot for her. She asked me to pray about the gunk they were breathing in. She was right to fear this.

My greatest fear was for Neil, for the man who tried to take his own life less than three months after the horrible day. How would he be with all the media attention focused on the day that devastated him? His e-mails told me the sad truth:

> *I've been in the dumps lately, with the anniversary coming up. It's not an anniversary. We're not celebrating! As you can see, I used the wrong word. The "Memorial" is coming up! I spent a few hours in Barnes & Nobles looking through a lot of 9-11 books. Remembering the areas I was in while searching for victims. I did not receive an invitation from Pelco and I really don't mind. I wouldn't come, due to the fact of what I attempted the last time. I thought about it and it's just too hard for me, to see all those empty chairs! I know I wouldn't hold up! It's the crying game.*

I had heard thousands of personal stories about 9/11, but Neil's story touched me the most. I thought his story was incredible, and I told him so. But nothing I said could make the day any easier. Shortly before the event, he wrote:

> *I'm a little in the dumps (no pun intended). Re: Staten Island dump. I'm trying to get off of work on 9-11, so I can be at the memorial at ground zero! I'm confused. I don't know if I really want to be there! I still cry till this day! I was in tears at work last night watching TV about the WTC. I was in a store the other day, looking through new books of the WTC. This woman asked me if I'm a fire fighter. I said yes. We conversed about that day and I started to well up! That was the end of that conversation!*

Neil ended this note with: "Thanks for listening. I mean reading." Maybe I could make the day a little easier for him. Just knowing that someone was listening, someone was carrying part of the hurt, could ease the pain enough to make it bearable.

I decided to do what I could to let other hurting heroes know that there were people who were carrying part of their suffering. On the eve of September 11, 2002, around ten p.m., I got on my computer and sent a message to all those in New York for whom I had an e-mail address. I put in the subject line the title "Midnight Oil." I knew many would be apprehensive as to what the next day would bring. Many would be unable to sleep. I thought some might be at their computer and might need a word of encouragement. So under the title "Midnight Oil," I sent a prayer and an assurance that someone knew their pain.

I got a few responses back. Most were like the one from "Uncle Vinnie" that began, "Thank you for this beautiful message. It touched me at this time when I need it."

A small touch can make a huge impact on someone who is hurting. A Federal Protective Service officer from Ohio named Michael Takacs e-mailed in for some memorial items. He had worked Ground Zero the month of December

2001. He was not engaged in the digging, but had been assigned there by his agency. I thought that since he spent a month at the site and had a job protecting people, he deserved one of Pelco's medals. So on September 10, 2002, I sent a hero's medal by Fed Ex overnight morning delivery to Michael. I wanted him to receive it on September 11.

It did arrive the morning of the first anniversary. It was a little thing for me to do, but it was a big lift for one who did so much. Mike wrote:

I can't even think right now, we do our job – we love what we do. Knowing that we are in your thoughts means the world. It is nice to know a company like PELCO remembers. I will honor the medal forever.

Pelco remembered in a big way. Long before the main ceremony began, the day's events opened at 5:30 a.m. with bagpipers playing *Amazing Grace*. It was surprising and touching to see approximately 1,000 people from the community at such an early hour for such a solemn event.

The commemoration in New York started much earlier – at one in the morning. It began with bagpipe and drum processions through each of the city boroughs: Bronx, Staten Island, Queens, Brooklyn, and Manhattan. All the marchers arrived at about six a.m. at Ground Zero, where Mayor Giuliani read the names of the 2,801 victims and the heroes of the terrorist attack.

At Pelco, the flag was lowered to half staff. A twelve-year-old Boy Scout played *Taps* on his bugle. At the close of this preliminary portion of the observance, I watched as many of the local people gathered around each one of the New York guests and just hugged them.

The main ceremony took place at noon. The Brownie Lady was there, escorted in and seated with the New York guests. The one-hour ceremony was much like the December 8, 2001, memorial except somewhat scaled down. Mr. McDonald's father, a Presbyterian minister, gave an opening prayer. Ann Whitehurst sang the *Star Spangled Banner* – not the usual minute-and-a-half version, but a very flamboyant rendition with all the verses. It was quite fitting and well done. Randy Deaver again sang *God Bless the USA*.

New York Port Authority Chief Anthony Whitaker gave a very gripping account of what happened to him on 9/11. I don't think anyone within earshot that day will forget his words:

It is fitting and proper that we gather here today in Clovis, California. I was here in December for the Memorial Dedication. At that point in time, just 90 days after the collapse of the World Trade Center, I was still very numb. As I traveled here last year, I did not know what to expect. But let me tell you, the warmth and love and support that I felt from this community nine months ago, and continue to feel, has given me the strength to carry on.

I worked at the World Trade Center. I loved the World Trade Center. It was a brilliantly conceived jewel of office space, public space, retail space and public transportation. IT IS NO MORE.

In many ways, the Towers will always be there … in our minds and our hearts. We must never forget. We will never forget. I am proud to say that for me, a very significant part of this remembering is here, in Clovis. I now have somewhere to go to reflect, to heal, to quietly sort out my feelings.

While the future of the World Trade Center complex is still in doubt, the cities of Clovis and Fresno … knew what needed to be done. The Memorial is a reality. The museum is a reality…

On September 11, 2001, I was the Commanding Officer of the World Trade Center Police. What began as a beautiful fall day became another painful "Day that Will Live in Infamy" for America. Like December 7th, 1941. Now we add September 11th, 2001. TWO TRAGIC DAYS IN AMERICAN HISTORY.

I was inside the World Trade Center complex when the first aircraft STRUCK the North Tower. I started to hear a strange roar. It grew in volume, getting louder until it felt like it was next to me, punching against the side of my face. I looked toward the entrance to the North Tower and I saw a huge fireball rolling out of the lobby. It looked like it was pushing people in front of it. It looked as if there were people all around the fireball, and as if there were even people inside of it – free-floating in the flames. I can't describe how horrible it was.

I dove into a hallway to take cover. I may have blacked out. I don't know how long I was there. When I finally came out of my daze, I struggled to my feet and walked back out into the main corridor. There was no light. There was no sound.

Then I saw two bright images moving toward me from the direction of the North Tower lobby. As they drew closer, I began to see that these lights were actually people running toward me – people on fire. They weren't saying anything, and I don't remember hearing even the slightest noise as they ran right past me. I couldn't tell if they were white, black, male or female. Just flames.

Outside the building, I walked past St. Nicholas Greek Orthodox Church. I heard a roar. A huge sucking sound. And the BOOM! It was the second aircraft coming into Tower Two. Another huge fireball blew out of the building and a heat wave pounded the side of my face as I ran and dove through an open door. There were explosions everywhere. People started screaming.

The explosions were caused by hot pieces of structural steel from Tower One flying through the air like toothpicks. The pieces of steel were so hot that when they struck a vehicle it would ignite the gasoline, causing the vehicle to explode.

God did me a favor by shutting off much of my memory of that day. There is still a great deal I do not remember. The parts I do remember are almost too much to bear. I know I'll carry them with me for the rest of my life. And I do not want to forget.

MANY HAVE BEEN LOST BUT NOT FORGOTTEN. We must never forget. ONE YEAR AGO TODAY, September 11th, 2001, "A DAY THAT WILL LIVE IN INFAMY."

The ceremony ended with the song *Wind Beneath My Wings,* a release of doves, and a 21-gun salute. After the crowd cleared a bit, I gathered some of the place cards from the chairs to send to friends. I was determined to find two in particular – Michael Bocchino for Neil Malone and Donald Burns for Vincent Medordi (Uncle Vinny). I found both.

For many who attended, this anniversary ceremony was like a welcome salve on still open wounds. For others, it was a fresh reminder of those unhealed wounds. On the day of the ceremony, new people called my office, needing someone to listen.

A woman from Sacramento wanted to talk about her friend who had been in the World Trade Center on that fateful day. The friend could not find her way out. She had made it to the ground floor but had to go back up one level through the fire and smoke in order to exit the building. She couldn't see which way to go. A fire fighter took her by the arm. With his other arm, he grabbed another woman and led the two of them out of the building to safety. He immediately turned around and went back into the flames. A few minutes later, the building collapsed. He saved two and gave his own life.

A woman whose nephew is a pilot called. The nephew normally flew one of the planes that crashed, but he had the day of September 11th off. Someone else called – someone who had a family member on one of the ill-fated planes. Two calls: one person saved, one lost.

A call came in from the family of a local fallen fire fighter. He had died as the result of an explosion just before the December 8th memorial ceremony. When the New York guests heard the story, they dipped deep into their pockets and raised several thousand dollars for the family in a matter of minutes. Such was the brotherhood of rescue workers ... and the generous hearts of true heroes.

Some of those hearts, however, I knew were breaking. I still worried about Neil's. Had he made it through the anniversary? On September 13th, I finally heard from him. He had "wanted to be with the 'guys' on this solemn day," he wrote, but he had to work instead. He said, "I watched the coverage all day, wishing I were there. After work, I went out with a few guys, drank a lot, told my story to three strangers, all the while crying! Sometime after midnight, I found my way back to the firehouse. I showered, went to bed, only to wake up that morning to work.

"At any rate," he ended his message, "I think I'm doing okay."

Maybe doing "okay" sounds somewhat defeatist. But for Neil, "okay" is good. It is hundreds of times better than he was doing nine months earlier.

CHAPTER 15

FDNY HERO #344

After the first-year anniversary of 9/11 passed, I should have been relieved. As far as I knew, everyone deeply scarred by the tragedy had made it through the commemoration ceremonies and reminders. The phone calls kept coming, but they were not as sad. They were mostly from surviving family members and those working the horrible but necessary jobs at Ground Zero. I sent hero medals to the ones who did not have the opportunity to come to California. Lots of e-mails were going back and forth. Many were expressing patriotic sentiments: prayers for our troops, tributes, the words to *Taps*, and information about the American flag. It was a time of great patriotism and pride in our country. It seemed as though people had begun the long, slow road to healing.

They were getting better because they were relying on one another. Pete Paolillo, the Florida fire fighter transplanted from New York, talked of a fellow fireman who had helped him. "If it was not for 9/11," he said, "I probably would not have met him. We were brothers before this happened, but we will be lifelong friends because of it."

Pete helped me understand something of how healing works … and why my telephone and e-mail contacts mattered:

> The tragedy on 9/11 devastated many families. But it also created new relationships and bonds between people that would have never been brought together. I guess that is the way we will all get through this and grow stronger together.

But concern for the 9/11 heroes still nagged at me, especially for Neil Malone. Was he getting through this? He had said he was "okay," but he did not say things were good. He had spent the anniversary crying. Was he really all right? Did he still feel responsible for the deaths of the 343 fire fighters who lost their lives that awful day? I had to find out. So, five days after the anniversary, I e-mailed him:

> I hope you are doing better today. I saved your friend Mikey's card from the chairs Wednesday. Let me know if you want me to send it to you. I have an address of a Tommy Bocchino in Pennsylvania. I noticed it the other day on one of my lists. Do you know if there is any relation? I kind of feel bad asking as I don't want to cause you to even think more at this time. But somehow I couldn't let the card pass. I saved

others for people I know after the NY guys that were here took the ones they wanted. Brighter days are coming. Take care, dude.

Neil wrote back, and at first his message seemed positive. It sounded cheerful and was punctuated with happy exclamation points:

Good Morning! Tommy is Michael's brother. I met Tommy at Michael's Memorial service soon after 9-11. I asked him for his address after I told him about Pelco's dedication! He said he had no idea that you did that for all the victims. I told him that you had put together a tape, CD, and a book of that day! So I believe I spoke to you on the phone about sending Tommy the package, and that's how you and I became E-mail buddies! I would love to have it, but Tommy is family!

But the last two sentences told me how much Neil and so many others were still hurting: *Tommy told me his parents want nothing to do with anything from that day! It's funny, I was just talking to Michael's picture last night and here you write me about his picture!*

His grief was so deep that he was talking to a picture. He was missing his friend so much. I was glad he kept contact with me, but when time passed between his messages, my heart would grow heavy with worry. On September 30, 2002, he sent the following e-mail:

Did you hear that on Wednesday, a fire fighter took his life? He was despondent over losing many friends from 9-11! He took a rifle to his chest! We consider him #344! He was buried on Saturday. And it continues!!! Sorry to give you bad news but maybe people on the west coast need to know! Thanks for being there when I needed someone to talk to.

One year after the terrorist attacks, New York fire fighter Gary Celentani took his life in front of a shrine he had built in his house. Neil ended his e-mail with a somber and troubling P.S.: *Remember what I told you about December? I would have been #344!*

Of course I remembered what he had told me. He had talked about his own despondency. He had said he did not want to live with the painful memories of that day. He had wished he were dead – had planned to kill himself. Now, reading his words about a fellow rescuer who had succeeded in committing suicide, I ached with fear about Neil's emotional state. I fired back an e-mail:

I'm so thankful you told me. I am so thankful that you are still alive. Your life has purpose. I don't know why so many died as they did, why such an awful thing happened. But for whatever reason, God chose that you are still alive. He loves you. True, he loved and still loves the guys that were lost. But you are still here and you are needed here. Your family needs you. You help others when they are in distress, injured, in a fire. You have saved many lives. You are a help to me.

Lord Jesus, I pray for my friend Neil right now. Give him the ability to see how much you love him. Give him the strength to keep going. Touch his heart right now, Lord, I pray. Fill him with your peace, love and joy. Place a hedge of protection around him right now and keep him safe. Thank you, Lord. Amen.

As I hit "send," my anxiety grew. I was about out of my mind with worry. My heart was in the pit of my stomach. Was he still on his computer? Was he okay? He had my phone numbers, but he had never called. What would he do if the pain again became unbearable?

I decided I needed to call him. Pelco had the phone numbers of all the heroes who had come to our first Memorial ceremony. I called one of Mr. McDonald's assistants and explained the dilemma. She immediately gave me Neil's numbers. I felt both relief and apprehension when he answered the phone.

I did not beat around the bush. "I was wondering if you were okay," I explained.

"So-so," Neil said.

I told him that his e-mail concerned me. He understood and tried to assure me he really was all right. He told me a little about Gary Celentani. He talked about his anger toward the family of the little boy he had met on August 5, 2001. He had reported what he could remember of that meeting to the FBI and the FDNY headquarters. We talked about a lot of things: the incident with the Moroccan family, his electrocution, problems of guys contemplating suicide. He told me that several had voiced thoughts about the possibility of ending their lives. To prevent them from following through on these thoughts, they were all kind of looking out for one another.

The conversation lasted about an hour and a half. I basically just listened. When we hung up, I wasn't totally convinced that he would be all right. But we had shared a laugh or two. I hoped it was enough to take the edge off his sadness, at least for a time.

Now, however, in addition to the concern about suicide, I had a new worry. Neil was very angry with the family of the Moroccan boy who seemed to know something about the attack a month before it happened. Neil wanted to get even with them. I couldn't let that stand unchallenged. I knew that bitterness and anger would devastate Neil's spirit every bit as much as suicide would devastate his body. I sent another e-mail:

I hope you get this before you go to work today and keep it with you. I'm praying for you. I hope you will find your strength in Christ, who loves you more than anyone else can. He knows everything. I understand the anger, but anger doesn't lead to anything good. I do hope you will put aside the thoughts of revenge. Leave that for our military, the FBI, but mostly to God. In the end, they will not get away with what they have done. God will make sure of it. Maybe good will come to that little boy's life. Maybe he'll always remember how you talked to him and how you helped him. Maybe this will make a difference when he is grown and he will turn away from the sins of his parents. He'll look back on 9/11 and the pain caused. He'll remember you. It can make a difference. Pray for him. If you do, God will bless you.

I could only hope he would take my words to heart.

CHAPTER 16

IAFF MEMORIAL 2002

Every year, the International Association of Fire Fighters (IAFF) holds a ceremony to remember all who died in the line of duty in the previous 12 months. In 2001, however, no memorial was held because so many had lost their lives in the 9/11 tragedy and recovery efforts were still underway. When the IAFF held its ceremony in 2002, the event received wide recognition. Over 50,000 fire fighters and their families converged on Madison Square Garden in New York for the memorial on October 12, 2002.

People came from as far away as Europe. A group of 20 fire fighters from Italy came to the United States through San Francisco. They stopped to visit the California Memorial at Pelco, traveled to another memorial in Denver, Colorado, and went on to Madison Square Garden. Heavy work demands meant that I was not able to show them around. One of my co-workers teased me, noting that I already had a number of e-mail pals who were fire fighters. I had enough boyfriends around the world, he joked, and I didn't need to add 20 from Italy!

I wondered if Neil Malone would be at the IAFF memorial. A couple days prior to the event, he was not doing particularly well:

I had a medical at FD headquarters yesterday. Was a little worried I wouldn't pass! Had an EKG, showed an inferior wall infarction! I had to see the MD stat!! He looked at the EKG and said "YOU'RE FINE!"

What a relief! Now, I go and have my blood pressure taken. That's a little high! After all is said and done, I see another MD. He looks at everything and says, your pressure is a little high! I told him of my injury, he was amazed! He told me I passed. What a relief!!

Then I went to see the psychiatrist. I broke down! He wants to see me again on the 17th!

Despite the worries over his physical and mental conditions, Neil did attend the IAFF ceremony. He wrote me about it that evening:

I was at the Memorial at Madison Square Garden. Very touching!!! Also went to a plaque dedication for Michael Bocchino afterwards. I spoke with his parents, brother Tom, and his sister. I told her and her parents what you and Pelco did for us! They were very impressed! Said they wished they knew about it. All would have come! Tom told me his father was depressed and that today was his first day out in a long time! So I went over to his parents and introduced myself. His mother remembered me! I sat with them for a long period telling them about Michael! They told me Michael never told them anything and that it was refreshing to hear all the stories! After all was said and done, they all embraced me and thanked me! I felt so good!!! They told me Michael will be buried sometime next week and asked if I'll be there! I told them I would even if I have to call in sick!

The IAFF ceremony and the plaque dedication seemed to cheer Neil. And yet, his message was tinged with sorrow. His best friend was to be buried ... a full year after his death. Forty friends lost, perhaps as many funerals, and they stretched out over at least twelve months. But he had written, "I felt so good!!!" Was he getting better?

A partial answer came in a phone call from Jerri Hoover, Executive Assistant in Engineering. Jerri almost never had occasion to call my department, so I was surprised to hear from her. Not nearly as surprised, however, as I was at her first words.

"Do you know a Neil Malone?" she asked.

Somewhat startled, I told her I did. How would someone in Engineering know Neil? And why was she calling me about him?

"Is he suicidal?" she asked.

A lump caught in my throat. "Yes ... Is he okay?"

All Jerri knew was that a local fire fighter had met Neil Malone at the IAFF ceremony at Madison Square Garden and wanted to get back in touch with him. The fire fighter, Casey Clark, attended a Bible study with a guy named Scott in Pelco's Engineering department. Casey asked Scott if he knew a nice Christian lady at Pelco who kept in touch with a Neil Malone.

Before long, Casey was on the phone. He was one of three fire fighters from Fresno who had gone to the IAFF event. Sitting alone in a restaurant in New York, he heard a loud "FRESNO!" and turned around into a great big bear hug! It was Neil Malone. Casey asked him how he was doing.

"A huge look of sadness comes over his face," Casey said. "I've never seen such sadness. He told me his story and how he came out to Pelco. He told me of his suicide attempt. Then he told me about this Christian woman at Pelco who he said has helped him through so much. He said you were praying for him."

That I was. I was praying for his mental, emotional, and spiritual well-being. For peace of mind and strength of spirit. I was praying for his healing.

"Sue," Casey said, "he called you his angel. He refers to you as his angel. He believes in your prayers for him."

This was a bit overwhelming for me! I didn't know I was having such a big and positive effect on Neil. All I wanted was to be an encouragement, a help wherever help was needed. I just didn't realize how big the need was. Or how powerful simple words of caring could be.

CHAPTER 17

USS ARIZONA – ALOHA

There is a flag that connects the east coast of the United States, the west coast, and the island state of Hawaii. It knits the hearts of people in those far-flung regions together … through the tragedy of 9/11. It also links the unprovoked attack on U.S. citizens with an eerily similar assault 60 years earlier.

The story of that flag begins with Mrs. Letitia Driscoll. She is the mother of Stephen, a New York police officer who gave his life that terrible day. Letitia called me often, usually with yet another list of names of people she wanted to receive our memorial books. She wanted to make sure all the NYPD families and everyone she knew had one of the books. She asked me to include my letter with my personal story with each package I sent. One of the names on one of her many lists was Skip Wheeler, an employee of the National Park Services in Hawaii.

Wheeler is connected with the USS Arizona National Memorial. The memorial is a 184-foot long monument that spans the midsection of the sunken battleship. Like the World Trade Center towers, the unsuspecting Arizona was hit by a fleet of airplanes early on a peaceful morning. In less than nine minutes, all 1,177 people on board were dead. In the surprise attack on Pearl Harbor, 2,388 Americans were killed – nearly 600 fewer than perished on September 11, 2001.

As a tribute to those 2,388, the United States flag flies from a pole that is attached to the severed mainmast of the submerged vessel. This flag has come to symbolize heroism in dedication to the service of our country. To honor heroes in other times and places, personnel at the Arizona Memorial fly a flag for only a few months then certify it and send it as a gift to a museum, organization, or individual that has demonstrated or celebrated such heroism. Skip Wheeler's job was to send the Arizona's flags to deserving people.

Letitia had received a certified flag from the Hawaii memorial. It was sent in memory of her son Stephen. The flag had arrived on July 4, 2002. The date was significant for Letitia for two reasons. It was the 226th birthday of the United States, and it would have been Stephen's 39th birthday.

Letitia had requested a second flag. It was to honor all 23 New York police officers who lost their lives on 9/11, including Stephen. When she received it, she and her husband presented it to the New York City Police Commissioner and it was placed in the New York City Police Museum as part of its September 11th exhibit. Letitia must have had difficulty parting with this particular flag. It had flown over the USS Arizona on Stephen's birthday. Wheeler, understanding Letitia's pain and her pride, handled her dilemma delicately. He told her that the flag in the museum would honor Stephen the police officer and the flag in her home would honor Stephen the son.

As my friend requested, I contacted Skip Wheeler. I sent him a package of our memorial items. He wrote back describing his correspondence with Letitia Driscoll. And he made a generous offer. Would the Pelco museum have the desire and the place for a certified flag that had flown over the USS Arizona? I was thrilled! None of us were heroes on the scale of the men entombed on the World War II ship or the rescuers of 9/11. But our remembering, encouraging, and honoring those who were was counted as heroic.

Skip wrote again when our flag was taken from its pole. He said he would have the certificates made and the flag would be on its way to us. He mentioned that Letitia Driscoll and her husband, "have been on a whirlwind mission since 9-11, going places and drumming up patriotic support – almost like the bond drives during WWII." He commented that, in some ways, the country hadn't changed. Americans still loved America, patriotism was alive and strong, and misfortune tightened the cords that bound us together.

When the flag arrived, there was an envelope in the box for me. It held a pin with the words "Live Aloha." I added it to my collection and added Skip to my growing list of friends. He was also a healer.

CHAPTER 18

TURNING POINTS

As 2002 drew to a close, I still worried about Neil Malone. When time lapsed between his messages, I wondered what might be going on. When the subject line read "Still Breathing," I caught my breath. When I heard any disturbing news from New York, I questioned how he was. I knew that November 3rd would be a challenge for him. It was the day the remains of his closest friend, Michael Bocchino, would be laid to rest.

Neil had wanted to be present when Michael's body was found so he could "take him home." At least he could be with him one last time. Neil looked forward to the funeral with both anguish and some pleasure. He was to be a pallbearer, which he considered a privilege and an honor. But he feared he might break down. "If I do, I don't care what people think," he wrote. "All I know is I loved Michael and I miss him dearly! We had many good times and I hope I retain those memories."

I didn't realize how deep those memories were until I received a package from Neil after the funeral. It contained, among other things, a program of the service and a brochure with pictures that catalogued his friend's life. Several of the photos, taken over a number of years, were of Michael and Neil together. Looking at those pictures, I understood what he meant when he said that he and Michael had "been there" for each other so many times.

The day turned out to be a turning point for Neil. "Since Michael's funeral, I feel different," he wrote. "Feels like a huge burden has been lifted! I'll be O.K."

He had apparently handled the responsibilities of pallbearer without going to pieces. He had even helped fold the flag that had draped his friend's coffin. He had stood tall as the flag was presented to Michael's parents. But he was a little shaken by a strange incident that occurred at the funeral home. Michael's sister, Debra, made a point of apologizing to Neil for not speaking to him the previous night. Neil thought that was odd, because he had not been with the family that evening. Yet Debra insisted that he was! After Michael's burial, his brother Thomas also mentioned Neil's presence the preceding night. Neil explained again that he was not there with them. Thomas called Debra's husband over and asked if he had seen Neil the night before and he replied that he had! Even after Neil had a fellow fire fighter confirm that they were working together that night, the family insisted that Neil had been with the Bocchino family. He decided that, although he was not there physically, he was with them spiritually.

I did not know what to make of the strange story, but I was heartened by Neil's obvious sense of release from some of his grief. When the funeral was over, he wrote, "I think this was the last chapter."

I congratulated him on holding up so well. "I hope life will become happy as you move on," I said. "Brighter days are coming."

I told him about a little boy who reminded me of him. He had come to my church's Harvest Fest a few days earlier in a fire fighter's costume. It was black with yellow stripes and said "FDNY." The boy's mother told me he would have no other costume. He refused to even look at anything else. It touched my heart that a little boy in California wanted to be like the New York heroes. I hoped it touched Neil's heart, too.

Neil's heart had begun to heal from one wound. Michael's funeral started that. But another gaping hurt continued to fester. Neil was still troubled by his December 2001 suicide attempt. He was embarrassed by the fact that he nearly let his pain and confusion ruin the wonderful thing Pelco had done for him and the others who fought so valiantly in the terrorist attack. He didn't mind anyone knowing the other parts of his story. The encounter with the Moroccan boy, the electrocution, and the fact that he had survived while so many didn't – these were things over which he had no control. But the pills in the motel room … he was ashamed of that. "The only thing I'm not proud of," he wrote me, "is my attempt to end my life. That wouldn't have been fair for the Pelco employees or Mr. McDonald. All of you have been so kind! As you know, I'm still hurting."

Yes, I knew he was still hurting. But I saw everything differently. I saw that lonely event as another turning point. I tried to tell him that:

I've been thinking. From everything you have been through this last year, I think it was good that you came out here. Even though it was probably your lowest point and so difficult for you, I think it was the beginning of your healing. Don't look back at December 8 as a low point, but as your transition point. That morning when the radio woke you, I believe God gave you a special message – and you heard. I believe since then you have continued to gain strength. You will continue.

I included a scripture for him, one of my favorites:

Isaiah 61 "The Spirit of the Lord is upon Me. Because the Lord has anointed Me to preach good tidings to the poor; He has sent Me to heal the brokenhearted, to proclaim liberty to the captives and the opening of the prison to those who are bound, to proclaim the acceptable year of the Lord and the day of vengeance of our God. To comfort all who mourn. To give beauty for ashes, strength for fear, gladness for mourning and peace for despair.

I thought that Neil had turned a corner and was beginning to experience some of that comfort and peace. After Michael's funeral, he sent some items to Mr. McDonald, president of Pelco. And he included a personal note. This was a huge step for him – sharing his private pain and his appreciation with a total stranger.

It turned out to be a huge moment for me, too. Not long after Neil's package arrived at Pelco, I was called into Mr. McDonald's office.

Being summoned to the office of the president of the company feels a little like being sent to the principal. I was terribly nervous. I had no idea what Neil had written or what Mr. McDonald was thinking. The first thing he said was, "What can you tell me about Neil Malone?"

I recited Neil's story as briefly as I could and told him a bit about our friendship. Touched, he said, "You probably saved his life." He knew that my job sending out the memorial books had put me in contact with a number of police and firemen. He also knew that some of those contacts had continued. I'm not sure he knew why. So I told him that many of the people I talked with were struggling just like Neil. I said that I believed that our concern for them might be saving their lives. Mr. McDonald said, "God sure put the right people in the right positions."

Mr. McDonald listened intently. I told him about how Tom O'Neill had called in for the memorial books and asked for a few minutes of my time. He simply wanted to tell someone his story. I told Mr. McDonald about my letter. He chuckled when I said that I sometimes sent prayers and jokes to Neil and the others. Then he explained the good he was trying to achieve with the memorial efforts. He appreciated what I was doing. When I told him I was following his lead, he said, "But you took it a bit far."

I looked down. Did he disapprove of all the correspondence that I thought was so important? "But they were so desperately hurting," I reasoned.

He instantly understood. "Don't ever change," he said.

I was overwhelmed! I had my boss's permission – his blessing – to continue to be part of the healing process for Neil and others like him. A funeral, a failed suicide attempt, a 45-minute conversation – each a turning point. And every turn was for the better.

CHAPTER 19

THE HOLIDAYS 2002

"Empathy is your pain I feel in my heart."

I always look forward to the Christmas holidays. I love decorating, sending cards, baking cookies and other goodies, and shopping. It's always so busy, but the joy all the preparation brings to my family and me is worth every minute of it. I know that I am creating special memories for my children.

But for those who have been through trauma, especially when that trauma involves great loss, those special memories can turn painful. The sea of merriment and good cheer can make one's personal sorrow even blacker. For many, just getting through the holidays can be a nightmare. I wondered about those on the east coast who were facing a second holiday season without their loved ones. How does a woman who lost her husband in a brutal, senseless attack find the strength to celebrate Christmas with and for her children? How does a parent get through the holidays without a beloved son or daughter?

I wondered, of course, about Neil Malone. After I told him about my chat with Mr. McDonald, he was quiet for a time. As time passed with little or no word, I grew increasingly concerned. I suggested to Diana Mather, Mr. McDonald's assistant, that it might be nice if Mr. McDonald gave Neil a call acknowledging his gift and card. I thought it might boost Neil's spirits if he heard from Mr. McDonald personally.

Mr. McDonald obliged my request, and Diana called Neil to arrange a conversation. But her phone call only reached his voice mail. He did not call back. Diana was persistent, and when she tracked him down he agreed to talk with Mr. McDonald. But Neil wrote to me:

> *In all honesty, I don't want to speak with anyone! I just want to be by myself! I'm going through a lot of highs and lows with the Holidays here. I might go see the shrink if I feel my self slipping deeper.*

Then he wrote of another struggle that began with 9/11:

> *I've been on the wagon for 25 days now! I will fall off! My wife told me she wishes I'd go back to drinking. I enjoy it very much, but I really don't miss it. After 15 months*

of boozing with two months of drugs included, I felt it was time to stop for now. I don't know why I tell you this. No, I do know. In the beginning, it was anonymous; I never thought we would be sharing pictures. That's when it became personal. I should have left it anonymous. Please don't feel sad, I do thank God for steering me in your direction. Because I most likely wouldn't be here if not for you! Thank you! As always thanks for listening!!!!

My heart sank. I felt so bad for him! He had told me about his struggle with alcohol, but I didn't know that drugs were also involved for a time. Thank God he didn't keep that up! To this day, he has not gone back to them. This was an eye-opener for me. It showed me how deeply he was still hurting. His wife and his kids must be in great pain, also. I told him I didn't think his wife really wanted him to go back to drinking, but she had watched him go through so much. I reminded him that she hurt with him. I told him my heart went out to her.

I put all the encouragement I could in a long e-mail, but I felt I needed to talk to him person to person. So I gave him a call. He was at work and he sounded happy to hear from me. During the course of the conversation, I heard a high-pitched sound in the background and I asked him what it was.

"Oh this?" he asked when the sound recurred. "This is our breathing apparatus. I'm testing them. It's what helps us breathe when we are in a burning building. This is the sound it makes when it's on and hasn't moved for 15 seconds. It's an alarm that lets us know when a fireman is down."

He started to get a bit choked up. *Strange*, I thought, *that describing a piece of equipment would make him emotional.* Strange, until he explained:

"This was all you heard that day. It was bad. It was real bad. I've seen your LA Watts. I've seen decapitations and body parts. This was worse. This was a lot worse! Guys kept taking off their breathing apparatus to help victims breathe. It was all you heard that day … It was all you heard."

He could barely go on. That sound that was in the background for me was in the forefront of his memory of "that day." It was the repeated and continual squeal that said one fireman after another was "down," not breathing, crushed under the weight of steel and concrete and bodies. I was at a loss for words! All I could say was that I was glad that he survived.

Until now I had not known that he was at the World Trade Center on 9/11. How could he have been there that day? He was barely out of the hospital recovering from being electrocuted! It was incomprehensible. But it explained the depth of his suffering. I choked back tears as I said simply, "I'm glad you talk to me."

"I'm glad I talk to you, too," Neil managed to say.

When we ended the phone call, I sat in silence for a long time. It ended on such a sad note that I was not sure he was going to be okay. My heart felt so heavy. Finally, I slipped to my knees and prayed, "Dear Lord, protect his life. Bring healing to him and his family." I called some friends who said they would pray for Neil, too.

It may seem unusual that I kept in such close contact with Neil. I just felt I had to keep him talking. I was pretty sure I was the only one he really was opening up to. If I didn't keep him talking, then who would? I could not think of abandoning him at this time. He would send me sad messages, then fill up my e-mail inbox with jokes. It was his way of coping with the sadness. So long as the messages kept coming in, I felt he was okay for today. I would breathe a sigh of relief. I noticed early on that he did not e-mail a lot of people. This made me feel that for some reason he needed to talk to me. Why it was me that he was opening up to was still a bit of a puzzle to me. He had begun to hint at the answer, but I would understand more over the next several months.

CHAPTER 20

HUNTING STICKERS

In January 2003, I had another occasion to write Neil. As a fundraiser for a 9/11 memorial, someone was selling "hunting stickers." These were somewhat humorous, each one claiming to be a permit for hunting terrorists. One was for California, one for New York, one for New Jersey and one for anywhere in the United States. I bought a set and sent the New York sticker to Neil. I told him I was hanging on to the California one.

Neil showed the one I sent him to several people, and he wanted to get additional ones for his friends. I was unsuccessful in providing them for him. When I wrote him about the stickers, I took the opportunity to ask how he was doing. I would always ask him if he was all right. Sometimes I asked how he felt about Mr. McDonald knowing his story. I still worried that he would be upset about it. I got the following message in reply:

> *Thanks for thinking of me. I do appreciate it! I haven't written because I've been in a low for awhile. I have a lot on my mind – what's left of it! I met a fire fighter from Manhattan two weeks ago. His name is Sal. He was one of the six that survived the WTC collapse! He was in the stairwell with his company (Ladder Company 6) and an elderly woman who couldn't walk another step. I'm sure you heard of this story. It was a special on* Dateline. *Anyway, I asked him if I could talk to him in private. I told him my story. I asked him not to have ill feelings towards me. He was very supportive! I found out the next day, he asked the two guys I was with to keep an eye on me! They kept calling my house and 'fessed up. He didn't tell them of our conversation. Sal kept his word! We both consider each other a Miracle! He said he doesn't blame me, which was great to hear! He couldn't believe what I told him. I told him about you and all you've done in helping me heal! I asked him to tell whoever, just as I asked you!*
>
> *My story needs to be told! I think you should … do it! By the way, it was me who told Mr. McDonald what my intention was, not you … So don't feel bad! My not writing you has nothing to do with any of this! When I'm depressed, I don't write anyone!*

I was beginning to wonder if he would ever be able to be free of the pain he was going through. Again, he had said I was helping him heal, but he still sounded so sad. If I was helping him, he still had a long way to go. My heart remained heavy.

Neil's suggestion – or rather, request – that I tell his story stuck in my mind. I had mulled over the idea before of writing about the effects of 9/11 on Pelco and me, perhaps even telling Neil's story. But my thought was that I would write it sometime in the future … a decade or two from now, looking back at this time in history … not now. But Neil had several times asked me to do it … write a book … tell his story. I had never written anything. Where would I start? If I did write a book, what effect would it have on Neil and others like him? I wanted to help the healing, not hinder it!

I thought of one of Pelco's writers who had been my friend for several years. She had once told me that she could help me write about my life as a survivor of hydrocephalus. I had always thought that would not be a particularly interesting read. But now I wondered if she could figure out what could be done for Neil.

Before I could write to her, though, I received an e-mail from none other than her! My manager at the time, Howard Carder, had told her I knew some fire fighters who wanted to tell their 9/11 experiences. She was contacting me to find out how she could help.

"I don't know what I'm in for," her e-mail said. "an article … a book, perhaps. I don't know, but I'd like to give it a try."

I wrote her back right away! "Yes, Yes, Yes! It will be a post-9/11 book."

I had notebooks of the conversations I'd had when people phoned my office. I was not taking notes for a book at the time; I just wanted to remember the people and what they said and felt. I would keep contact with some of them and I would pray for most. I believe my contact with them was God extending His hand to them. It was my job to listen. I also kept all the e-mails I received relating to 9/11, and by this time, they numbered in the thousands. Neil had told me, "You won't be profiting from the suffering of others. You will be helping to tell the story."

I was excited about the possibility of putting all this in print. I wrote to Neil. "I have told my boss about you and others," I began. "He keeps tabs on me and all this stuff. But I told him this morning what you said to me in your last e-mail, about writing your story, a book on 9/11. How you have mentioned this several times."

I explained that my good friend and fellow Christian was willing to help tell the story. "She has had articles published before in magazines and is one of Pelco's writers," I said. "She knows how to approach publishers."

That evening I received a call. Neil was on the other end. His first words were, "So, do you think it will be a bestseller?"

CHAPTER 21

BECOMING REAL

For a few months after our first serious conversations about telling his story in a book, Neil was very quiet. I wondered if he was having second thoughts about sharing his story with so many others. Was he worried about what people might think? Did he not want his experiences in print after all? I didn't care so much about the book; I just did not want to not lose my connection with him. I sensed he still needed someone to talk to.   Sometimes I would question whether I should continue communicating with him. Was my listening ear really helping him heal? Maybe I was being a pest. Maybe I should just leave him alone to live his life. Most mature, proper, married women don't keep writing to a man they don't know very well.

But for some reason, Neil was on my heart. It was a deep concern, not an attraction. I have always believed that God places one person on another's heart for a reason. We may not understand what the reason is, but our job is to pray for the ones God puts on our hearts and help them any way we can. It is a means of "standing in the gap" between them and whatever evil or negative thing is troubling them. I did that for Neil. I lifted his name up in prayer, asking God to work miracles in his life.

And as Neil took little steps toward health, I saw some of those miracles. He acknowledged them, too. On March 19, 2003, I e-mailed Neil, reminding him that he had first spoken to me exactly one year earlier. He had not recalled the date. "But then again," he wrote, "I don't know much from that period. Perhaps it's because I don't want to remember that time of my life! I believe you saved my life!!! As you know, I was on a downward spiral … I've come a long way, wouldn't you agree?"

Yes, he had definitely come a long way!

But he, and indeed our country, still had a long way to go toward healing. To facilitate that process and again honor the heroes who gave their lives in the fight against terrorism, Pelco planned another memorial ceremony at our facility in Orangeburg, New York. The ceremony, scheduled for June 2003, was to be much like the one we had held on December 8, 2001, in California. The trip to the ceremony was open to Pelco employees and local fire fighters and policemen just as the Saint Patrick's Day trip had been.

I did not have to think twice; I was going. As the trip grew close, however, I learned that my father's girlfriend was planning a big birthday party for my father on the same weekend I had planned on being in New York. I was torn, but I wanted so much to meet the people with whom I had been corresponding. I decided my dad would likely have other birthdays, but I might not have another chance to see my heroes – America's heroes.

I started to contact all my New York friends, letting them know I would be coming and I wanted to meet each one of them! It wasn't long before they responded. Tom O'Neill had planned on attending a reunion of the naval unit he was in during the time of the Vietnam war. Tom served on the U.S.S. *Plymouth Rock* LSD29. This unit did not go to Vietnam, but rather were in combat in Santa Domingo during an attempted communist takeover. He cancelled his plans for that event because I was coming to New York! Tom and his wife wanted me to invite other Californians to a firehouse two blocks from their home, Engine 167 Ladder 87. They wanted to cook a meal for us there.

Letitia Driscoll wanted to set up a time for me to visit with her and her daughter Gail. Mrs. Driscoll left a long, emotional message on my voicemail. "I can't wait to meet you!" she gushed. Gail asked if I would consider spending a night at her house.

Tim Keenan was beside himself. "You're coming to New York?" He exclaimed when I told him. "YOU are coming to New York! What do you want to do? Would you like to go out to dinner? Would you like dinner at the firehouse? What? We have to get together!"

I was so surprised and happy to hear such warm welcome from so many. I was really beginning to look forward to the trip! There were so many I hoped to meet, many I knew by voice or e-mail only! But of them all, Neil remained silent.

I, however, was exceptionally busy. In early June, shortly before the trip for the Orangeburg memorial, Pelco celebrated its sixteenth anniversary. Each year on the day of the anniversary, employees gather for a celebration with cake and punch and a special speech from Mr. McDonald. About a week before, I had finally gotten up enough nerve to present the book idea to Mr. McDonald. I had written an outline and sent it with a letter in the interoffice mail. After a couple days, I received a voicemail from his executive assistant: "Mr. McDonald says this sounds like a pleasant project and said you should proceed." I was elated!

At the anniversary festivities, after Mr. McDonald's speech, I made my way slowly toward him. He was talking with a couple of ladies who work in production. As I approached, he paused in his talking with others, pointed to me, and said, "She's writing a book!"

I told our president, "I'm glad you are pleased with my plan to write a book. This trip to New York is important to me for this reason."

He replied, "I've been thinking that something like this needed to be done, and you are the one to do it." I was overwhelmed by his affirmation and the honor of telling the story of how a group of people in California was helping the heroes of 9/11 to heal!

Immediately, the missing pieces began to fall into place. Neadly Foster gave me a big hug and offered to be my cameraman. He had already told me that when we went to New York, he would be following me because I knew a lot of people there. He and our friend Eric Duffy would help me find my way around the Big Apple and get pictures for the book. I hoped that at least one of those pictures would be of Neil Malone.

Neil finally called and asked when I would be in New York. He told me to take all his phone numbers with me and promised that we would meet up somewhere. But he seemed nervous when we spoke about meeting. That nervousness was out of character for him. At first, I surmised that attending a ceremony that was much like the December 8th one might be tough on him. It would probably be a painful reminder of his suicide attempt. But it turned out that another ceremony was not the major problem.

Neil was nervous about meeting me. So far, I had been a faceless voice he could tell his story to. I was an encouraging word, a listening ear, a shoulder to cry on … a sort of disembodied counselor. He needed all those things because firemen have to be tough. They cannot do their jobs if they are immobilized by grief or fear or despair. Yet they need outlets for those emotions. Talking with me was a safe outlet for Neil; I was an e-mail address thousands of miles away, so he could tell me things about himself he dared not say to a real person. But then we exchanged pictures, and I became a little more real. Now I was going to add flesh to the picture. Neil wasn't sure he could handle meeting someone who could reflect back to him the most tortured parts of his last two years.

CHAPTER 22

MEETING OLD FRIENDS
FOR THE FIRST TIME

The morning dawned cool and slightly drizzly. But my heart was warm and bright; I was excited to leave for New York a second time. I had so much going through my mind, anticipating who I would meet and when. I didn't sign up for the various group events because I wanted to reserve as much time as I could for getting together with my New York friends. I knew the plans with Letitia and her daughter Gail were set. Plans to meet with the O'Neill's were in place. Plans with the guys of Ladder 123 were all ready. But with Neil, nothing had been arranged.

After the long flight, a phone message was waiting for me at the hotel. It was one of Letitia's daughters welcoming me to New York. I sensed I was going to be very busy and would have to guard against filling up my schedule. I needed to set something up with Neil before my few days on the east coast were too packed. I dialed his cell phone and left a message. He called right back. He seemed nervous … he wasn't sure he could get together with me. He just kept saying, "I don't know."

I had to fight back tears. This was the guy I had prayed for so much. This was the one I most wanted to meet. All night, I tossed and turned and wept just thinking of how hard life was for him right now. At dinner on our first night in New York, Eric Duffy reminded me, "You can't make him heal."

So on my first full day back in New York, I concentrated on my other friends. Our little group – Neadly, Eric and his wife Patty, and I – spent the time with Tom O'Neill, Fire Department Communications Technician on Staten Island. He gave us a tour of one of the dispatch facilities, then took us to a place called the Abba House. This is a Catholic Church that has a shrine to Our Lady of Perpetual Help. Tom told us that people had gathered here to pray when the 9/11 attack happened. "People were on their knees everywhere," he said. "There were so many people there was no room for more."

The place had a beautiful garden filled with candles and shrines. The main shrine had a large statue of Mary. It was like a small shelter. The walls were covered with pictures, prayer cards, and notes to loved ones lost. It took my breath away. Some benches were positioned in a kind of circle so that people could rest and maybe meditate.

A young man was sitting on one of the benches. He was obviously a fire fighter. He was wearing a shirt that said "Rescue 5." He sort of eyed us but didn't speak. He was clearly caught up in thought. I knew he must be hurting deeply. I wanted to talk to him and yet didn't want to offend or disturb him. I think we all felt the same way – not wanting to get in his way. It made my heart sink.

Tom then took us briefly inside the Abba House, where people kneel and pray silently and light candles. I was glad I was there. It made me feel I was sharing just a little in the rescuers' suffering and reminded me that I was also helping in the healing.

From this place of quiet refuge, we went to Tom's house. He didn't want to make his wife mad by arriving late! He told us we would also be visiting the guys at Engine 167 Ladder 87 just a couple blocks from his house. Over a fabulous dinner of salad and ravioli with sausages and garlic bread, we met Tom's wife Fran and their two talkative parakeets. FDNY artist Steve White stopped in for a brief visit. We looked through Tom's 9/11 books and marveled over Fran's ceramics.

Then Tom took us to the firehouse down the street. We had a wonderful tour of Engine 167 Ladder 87. We were allowed to try on the turnouts and Neadly and Eric slid down the pole.

Tom took us back to his house, where we had dessert with him and Fran and their daughter Michelle. Fran asked me to tell Michelle about my medical history. Michelle doesn't believe in God, but Fran wants her to think about Him. I told my story briefly, and I showed Fran and Michelle my scars and the dent in the back of my head. "You could fit a walnut in there!" Fran exclaimed. Fran told Michelle to read my letter I sent them. Michelle promised to read my story in the letter I had sent Tom and Fran and to think things over about faith.

The next day was also going to be jam-packed. But I was determined not to leave the city without meeting Neil. So I gave him a call first thing in the morning. He agreed to come to the restaurant where I was to meet Letitia and Gail for lunch!

When we arrived, the women were waiting for us. And they weren't the only ones. Dan D'Allara was there also. I was so happy to see all of them! But Neil was nowhere to be seen. Would he change his mind? I was afraid he might. I situated myself where I could see every new arrival.

Before too long, I spotted a guy with very dark hair in a red shirt coming our way. I knew instantly that it was Neil. I got up and gave him a hug right away! I couldn't believe he was actually there. He sat next to me and we all ordered.

I could tell this was difficult for Neil. He was chatting with everyone, but it was obviously painful for him. He excused himself to go to the bar. "Sue, I'm sorry," he said, "but I need a drink to get through this."

While he was away, other fire fighters joined us: Tim Keenan, Pat Burns, and Kevin Michaels. When Neil returned, he seemed a bit cold toward the other firemen. He turned to me and told me he was having a hard time. "It's the reason we are all here," he admitted.

I understood. This was yet another reminder of that awful day. I tried to replace the negative memory with a positive thought. "I'm so glad you are here," I told him. "I'm so happy to meet you! You've made my whole trip. Meeting you makes my trip complete." I meant it and saying it seemed to help.

When the meal was over, Tim, Pat, and Kevin pointed to their waiting Fire Department van. They asked if we wanted to go on a fire boat ride. We were all ready … all except Neil. "I have to head back," he said. But he had a hint of a smile on his face. "Uh … you can call me later," he offered.

Before he could get away, I said, "You know … there is one thing I haven't heard yet the whole time I've been here." I didn't have to explain. In less than a minute he feigned his Brooklyn accent.

"How yew doin'?" he said with a grin. He gave me a hug as he left.

At Marine 1, we were given a tour of the boathouse. Dan D'Allara exclaimed, "Just look at the ceilings! These are tin ceilings. Must be from the 20s!" On the wall was "The Flag of Heroes," prominently displaying the names of all the fire fighters and police killed on 9/11. The names are written on the red stripes.

Leaving the boathouse and the rotting wooden pier behind, we boarded the boat. The fire fighters who arranged this for us and who were accompanying us had never been on a fire boat themselves. They seemed as thrilled as we were for the experience. The boat took us all around the Bay. We saw the port where the Titanic was supposed to dock. We stood at the bow of the boat and Eric posed himself à la the hero in the *Titanic* movie and proclaimed, "I'm king of the world!"

Letitia, Gail, and I talked for a while on the cool and misty deck. They asked me about my mysterious friend, Neil. "He's handsome, but he has such sad eyes," Letitia observed. When they heard a bit of his story, they understood.

When we left Marine 1, we made our way to the firehouse known as Engine 234 Ladder 123 – St. John's East. I was introduced to the battalion chief on duty – Chief Steve Zaderiko. Our conversation was interrupted just minutes after our arrival as the station received a call. I had the awesome privilege of riding with them to that call. I stayed in the vehicle and watched them at work, not wanting to get in their way. This one was basically a false alarm; we were back at the firehouse in about ten minutes.

I told Chief Zaderiko a bit of the Pelco story and how the terrorist attacks had affected me and so many at Pelco. I mentioned the letter I had written to many of the fire fighters and police and explained why I wrote it. He was very understanding of my mission to gather information first-hand about how the rescuers were healing. He told me, "The Fire Department loses on average seven or eight guys a year in the line of duty. It's something we learn to live with."

It was hard for me to imagine living with the loss of seven or eight friends every year. What about the loss of more than 300 in one day? Would Neil and the others ever learn to live with that?

I didn't have long to think about it, because a call came in. I grabbed my camera and tape recorder and headed with them toward the action. When we arrived at the house, the guys brought out all kinds of equipment and did their search. Chief Zaderiko invited me to get out of the vehicle, stand on the sidewalk, and watch what was going on. He maintained communication with dispatch and still managed to explain to me what was happening. Many rigs showed up. Lines were drawn out. Guys were circling the building. Some were going in. We were there approximately twenty minutes. The fire turned out to be a pot in a kitchen.

Once back at the firehouse, I got to watch Tim Keenan conduct some training. He was instructing some of the guys as they practiced getting a locked door open. Quite an operation! I met Chief Phil Gaetani, who used to head up Ladder 123 and was now one of the safety chiefs for the city. He joined us for dinner. I felt so honored to be eating with these brave men, even though I had just met them.

The honor quickly turned to camaraderie when Chief Gaetani asked me to grab some ice cream from the firehouse's freezer. When I opened the freezer door, something wriggly and furry fell out! They had set me up! They were sort of initiating me into their group and I was thrilled. I didn't jump, I didn't scream. I had to explain, "Guys, I have four kids at home. Two are teenagers and I'm used to tricks."

Chief Gaetani laughed with everyone else. His driver had come to Pelco's December 8th ceremony. He had tried to get medals like the one he received there for two friends who hadn't been able to attend. He had called our Orangeburg location and was told he couldn't get any more. I told him I'd try to see if I could get him a couple.

In the meantime, I had items for all the guys at the station – shirts, hats, Pelco pins. I was giving things out to people as I met them. In return, Tim Keenan had some shirts for me!

Chief Gaetani and his driver drove me to my hotel in the Battalion Chief's vehicle. I couldn't believe their awesome treatment of me!

On the drive home, I told the chief that I had spent a lot of time on the phone listening to stories from the 9/11 heroes. "Yeah," he commented, "everyone in this business has a story."

I explained that I had come to New York to meet friends I had come to know through this experience. "I had to come," I told him. "I came for three reasons: Letitia Driscoll, Tom O'Neill, and Neil Malone."

"Neil Malone!" Chief Gaetani exclaimed. "You know Neil? Now there is a guy who can tell you stories!" He paused for a moment and then asked, "How is he doing, by the way?"

Not wanting to say anything Neil might not want revealed, I simply said, "He could do better." If he knew Neil well, that would tell him enough.

CHAPTER 23

FROM SEA TO SHINING SEA

Today was the day. Today was the memorial ceremony – the big finale for the New York weekend. Would Neil come? Did meeting me the day before calm his nerves and remove some hindrances? Or did it bring up too many painful memories? I hoped he would come.

Who else might I see today that I've wanted to meet? I called Vincent Petrucelli, who has the *Bravest Memorial* website. "I'm going to try to be there," he said. "Look for me – I'm about six-two with a bald head. I'm forty-one years old."

A lot of guys fit this description, I thought. I'll probably be going up to a lot of people asking if they are Vinny. I called Neil. "I'm just on my way out the door," he said. "I'll see you there." This was a great joy to me!

When everyone in the Pelco group gathered for the bus ride to the Orangeburg warehouse, we saw police officers and police vehicles everywhere. They rode in front of the limousine carrying Mr. McDonald, behind the limo, and behind the bus. We had a police escort the whole way. We were amazed to see how many drivers didn't care that police cars were accompanying us. Other drivers kept trying to cut in! This provided those of us on the bus a lot of entertainment!

I had barely stepped off the bus in Orangeburg when a couple came up to me. The couple had a son who is an NYPD officer. Their son had come to our December 8th ceremony. A month or so earlier, the gentleman had called me and told me his son's story. Then he sent me a package with pictures of his son, a Medal Day book, and some other items. I was touched then and doubly touched now that he and his wife were looking for me! They introduced themselves and their son to me. I was overwhelmed to think that brief conversations could mean so much when families are hurting.

Through the crowds of people from the police department, the fire department, and the Port Authority, I looked around to see if Neil was there. He was! And he was looking for me! He came up to me and hugged me, saying he wanted me to meet his brother, who was also there. "I may come to the barbecue afterwards," he said.

I really wanted him to come to the barbecue. I thought the more Pelco people he could meet, the less would be his misplaced sense of failing them by almost ruining their memorial. The more he saw that people appreciated him and understood his grief, the better he would feel. But tickets for the barbecue were limited. I immediately sought out Tim Glines, introduced Neil to him, and asked, "Would I be able to get a ticket for him?" Tim said, "No," but he smiled while handing me a ticket.

At some point, Neil told me, "Do me one favor. Don't introduce me to anyone." My heart sank. I wanted him to meet Mr. McDonald. I knew it would help Neil so much if he would talk with our president. But now there was no way for me to put the two together. I would not go against Neil's wishes.

Neil introduced me to his brother, Lt. Brian Malone. Now retired, Brian is a bit taller than Neil and slightly slimmer. I also met Neil's three best friends. Together, they were like the four musketeers.

Our visit was cut short when Neil and his friends had to line up with the rest of the fire fighters and police for the ceremony. I walked through the crowd, trying to find people I knew. Dan D'Allara was there with Carol, the widow of Dan's brother John. Carol had her small boys with her. I remember receiving a special NYPD publication that contained stories and pictures of many of the 9/11 widows and their children. This was the first time I saw Carol and her little ones. The sight brought home to me how great the losses so many families suffered were. Here she was. I got to speak with her only briefly.

I stood with Letitia Driscoll while the wife of an NYPD officer sang the national anthem. Letitia was so happy to see my friends and me, but she nearly buckled with emotion during the song.

I excused myself and moved toward the side where the fire fighters and police were standing. There were still so many I wanted to find – friends I had made over the telephone and e-mail.

I spotted someone who had become a dear friend even though I had not met him in person. From his picture from our December 8th memorial, his face and bearing were unmistakable. He is a thin, tall, handsome black fire fighter, around forty years of age. I remembered our first phone conversation when he called in for more copies of his picture that appears in our memorial book. We could have gone on and on talking at the time, but I had to work and he had promised to take his kids roller skating. He had become an e-mail pal. Now I was finally meeting him face to face – Van Don Williams, the man who had knelt between the rows of chairs to pray. I introduced myself.

Van Don was in the front row close to the end. He hugged me and apologized for writing so infrequently. "I get so busy," he explained. "But I see your messages come in and I always say, 'There she is, my sister in Christ.'"

When the ceremony started, I kept my eyes on Neil and his friends. I worried whether Neil would get through this memorial. I kept a close eye on him. Somehow, he made it through.

At the end of the ceremony, Neil invited me to ride with him and his friends Eileen and Buddy to the barbecue! We all walked the few blocks to where the car was parked. On the way, we passed two ladder trucks positioned with their ladders extended toward each other. These two ladders were picked because one was Ladder 9 and the other was Ladder 11. Proudly displayed between the two was an American flag.

On the ride, Neil seemed to loosen up a little. He teased his good friends. He called Buddy "SARS" when he coughed and "Skunk" because his grey roots showed in the part of his dyed-black hair. When drivers cut Eileen off, which happened more than once, Neil and Buddy goaded her, "Give them the finger, Eileen. Give them the finger." Eileen was known for her dislike of anything off-color; she made her department buddies give her a dollar every time they used language she considered offensive, and she donated the money to the Elsasser fund. So when teased by her friends, Eileen said, "Okay," and gave them her index finger.

Buddy said, "No, Eileen. Really give them the finger." So Eileen held up her thumb.

"And if I'm really mad," she told me, "they get all five." She held up her whole hand.

I was so glad that Neil had good friends like these. He seemed to be genuinely having a good time. He had a scrapbook he was going to show me, but decided to bring it out at another time. He gave me a bag of shirts from the firehouse for me and my friends. I was overjoyed!

As we walked from the car to the barbecue site, Neil kept warning me, "Watch your step ... Look out for that ... Don't trip." He was so attentive. I knew nothing was going to happen to me as long as I was with him!

In fact, he was watching after me so closely that he was not watching out for himself. Very suddenly, he slipped in some mud! He went all the way down, doing the complete splits. I grabbed his arm to try to help him up. His friend behind us said to Neil, "Okay, now try to talk!"

Neil started to ramble in a very high-pitched voice. It was absolutely hysterical! He managed to get up and he laughed, saying, "I'm glad for these new polyester uniform pants! Our old ones were wool. They would have split for sure."

At the barbecue, a number of people joined us at our table. One was our Fresno mayor, Alan Autry, who also happens to be a former television actor. Another was Mr. McDonald and his soon-to-be wife. Everyone was open and friendly and seemed to be enjoying themselves … Everybody but Neil. Neil placed himself where he would not be drawn into conversation. He got food, drinks, refills for people, but he did not enter into any table talk. He was so hospitable, acting as a host rather than a guest.

At one point, Mr. McDonald was directly behind Neil. Neil knew he was there, but he seemed to just freeze in place. I saw Mr. McDonald gently tap Neil on the shoulder in an effort to get his attention. Neil did not budge. He would not turn around, and Mr. McDonald did not press him. I held my breath and thought to myself, "Come on, Neil. Turn around! It's all right. You'll be glad you did. It will help you to talk to him. Turn around and talk to him!" But it wasn't going to happen and I would not go against Neil's wishes. If he was going to face Mr. McDonald, he would have to do so willingly, when he was ready.

I understood Neil's reluctance. He greatly admired Mr. McDonald and appreciated all he had done for the 9/11 rescuers. But he felt so bad about his suicide attempt during the December 8, 2001, weekend that he just couldn't bring himself to face Mr. McDonald. I know that no one – least of all Mr. McDonald – holds anything against him. We all understand the immense pain of tragedy. No one can pass judgment on another for how that person feels at such a time.

I turned to Neil's brother. "Neil told me he always wanted to be a fire fighter," I said.

"That is true!" Brian Malone replied. "Ever since he was small, it is all he ever wanted to do. I think he came out of our mom's womb wanting to be a fire fighter."

All the more reason, I thought, *that he needs to heal. He was born to be a fire fighter and he must continue to be a fire fighter. It's who he is.*

Our time together ended far too quickly. Before he left, Neil promised he would see me again before I departed for California. I wondered if he would. And he did one more thing before leaving. My friends Eric and Patty were making a video of New York guys saying "How yew doin?'" Neil does it so well. They got him to perform for the camera. Then he was gone.

But the party was not over. I had a chance to visit with Dan D'Allara again. He shared some deep thoughts about faith and what Pelco had done for him personally. He was impressed that a company that was not a rescue service would put so much into honoring, helping, and celebrating the New York rescuers.

I also talked with a fire fighter who had won the friendships of many on the west coast. Everyone's heart had gone out to him because of his youth and the effect of 9/11 on him. Andy Isolano had been forced to retire from the FDNY due to breathing problems.

Another young person there was the daughter of Tom Zinn of the Clovis, California Fire Department. She was missing her high school graduation to come on this trip. Tom had arranged with the NYPD Emerald Society a very special surprise for her. He and his wife had secretly brought a cap and gown and her diploma to New York. The Emerald Society presented the diploma to her! Then Tom danced with his daughter while the Pipes and Drums played. Tom's daughter was so touched she was in tears.

After the barbecue, back at the hotel, I called Neil's house. He wasn't home, but his wife answered. This was my first conversation with her! I was so glad for the chance to chat because I didn't know how she would feel about my friendship with her husband. I was surprised that she and her children had not come to the ceremony. Knowing how badly he hurt, I thought they'd want to be there with him. But they weren't. I wondered why. I know they have hurt with him. Her one comment to me told me so much. "It's hard to make my Neily smile," she said. That spoke volumes to me! It told me she loves him and she hurts for him. The conversation was a big relief for me because I felt I could be her friend as well.

The next day was Father's Day, and I decided not to disturb any of my New York friends on that day. I called my husband and children Saturday night. On Sunday, Neadly and I got lost in Central Park, then found a museum Chief Zaderiko had told us about. We were looking for a display of pictures by Gary Suson, Ground Zero photographer. We couldn't find the exhibit, but we found a theater room that was running a film with pictures of the 9/11 attacks and people giving their personal testimonies of that devastating event. The film brought tears to my eyes.

The film brought back conversations of the last few days. When I met the fire fighters from Ladder 123, Tim Keenan told me that there had been a 9/11-related funeral the day we arrived and another on the day of Pelco's memorial ceremony. This nearly two years after the tragedy! Tim also told me that remains were still being examined. At the barbecue, Dan D'Allara touched on that fact as well.

It had bothered me that I had not cried at the 2001 memorial at Pelco. I was sad about what had happened, but I had not shed a tear. Now, however, I had become so involved with so many who had been personally affected by the tragedy. The faces of those who were killed were becoming familiar to me even though I had never met them. I had gotten to know them through their families. Now, watching this film, I couldn't hold back the tears. I cried for Marcella Leahy, who lost her husband and for Letitia Driscoll, who lost her son. I wept for Carol D'Allara, who was raising three small children alone except for the help of her brother-in-law. For Stan Aviles, Peter Gale, and Tom O'Neill, who lived with the memories of fallen comrades. For Andy Isolano, who could no longer work. I cried for Ira Rosenberg and Rita Agnello, who had buried their sons. And I cried for Neil.

When I told my friend Casey Clark that I was happy that I was forming a friendship with Neil's wife, Casey warned me, "You don't want to lose Neil's trust." I understood. So many fire fighters and policemen have kept the depth of their hurt from their families. They don't want their loved ones to know what they go through. They want to protect their families from that knowledge so they won't worry. Sometimes, that fierce protection can push their families away. Some of these brave men, like Neil, were able to share their pain with me. I was far away, removed, so it was safe to talk with me. I would not hurt like their families would. This put me in a delicate position. As an anonymous ear, I was an outlet for their grief. Neil told me he wished I would have remained anonymous. But once I had a face, I was a real person who could be hurt. Sharing was not quite as safe then. Talking with Neil's wife made me even more real.

That night, the night before we left, I gave Neil a call to wish him Happy Father's Day and tell him farewell. He had spent his Father's Day installing air conditioning units in the upstairs bedrooms of his home. His family had taken him out to dinner. He said they had wondered where I was and why I had not contacted them. We talked for a long time. We talked about the book he wanted me to write. We joked about his fall at the barbecue. He asked, "What are you going to remember most about this trip? The fire boat ride? No. Meeting me? No. Me doing the splits? Yes!"

He told me again how difficult it was to meet me at the restaurant. And how hard it was to see Dan, Letitia and Gail, Tim, Pat, and Kevin, knowing that their family members died in an attack he thought he should have prevented. "It was terrible," he repeated. "It was so hard. It was why we were all there … I feel responsible for the loss of their loved ones. What would they think of me if they knew about me and what I knew?"

I tried to convince him that he didn't know enough to stop anything. The CIA and the FBI knew more than he and they didn't stop the attacks. "You knew something was coming, but you didn't know what," I reminded him. "There was nothing you could have done to prevent it."

"This is what people tell me," he insisted. "The psychologist told me the same thing. It doesn't matter. I still feel guilty. I feel I had some knowledge. I should have caused a fight with the father of the boy or *something*. I should have done *something*."

Then I remembered my conversation with Letitia and her daughter on the fire boat. I had told them part of Neil's story. They knew about the boy and they did not blame Neil for anything. "They knew when they saw you at the ceremony in Orangeburg," I said. "They knew when they hugged you there. They knew and they greeted you with open arms."

I hoped that those open arms, like my listening ear, would be part of his healing.

CHAPTER 24

FREEDOM'S FLAME AND FIRE MUSTERS

Neil was much different since we met face to face – pleasantly so. Even though to this day he will say he wishes I had remained somewhat anonymous, that meeting me made it harder for him to open up to me, he actually seemed to be much more open. He called often. We laughed often. We exchanged more jokes than ever! I think meeting me face to face had really done him some good. I was now a real person to him. And he realized he could share his real feelings with a real person.

After the trip, I learned of a group of fire fighters in Rancho Cucamonga, California who are creating a large monument in honor of the heroes of 9/11. The monument is to be called *Freedom's Flame*. The group has secured one of the engines damaged beyond repair in the recovery operations at Ground Zero along with a long piece of steel from the World Trade Center. To raise funds for the memorial, the fire fighters went on tour through thirteen states.

The completed memorial will be a 35-foot-tall monument that will have a sundial as its base. Around the sundial, different moments of the day of 9/11/01 will be documented. From the base, a spiral staircase will rise in the form of a flame, and figures will be placed at various spots on the stairs: civilians being helped down the stairs while fire fighters are going up. One fire fighter will disappear in the flame at the top. Very impressive!

When Rancho Cucamonga fire fighters came to Fresno, Pelco hosted them. The Clovis Fire Department and California Department of Forestry welcomed them. Neadly, Eric, and I were asked to be tour guides, available to answer any questions and to see to any needs of the guests. They came in the middle of summer. Summers in the San Joaquin Valley are always very hot. Temperatures can soar to as high as 116 degrees. We who live in this desert valley are a bit comforted to know that places in Arizona and Death Valley get a little hotter! On the day our guests arrived, the thermometer read 105.

Despite the heat, it was a wonderful visit. We showed the firemen our museum and took pictures with them by their trucks and by our monument. Tim Glines takes such opportunities to show off his antique car. It's always a special treat to see. He drove up with bags of gifts for the guests. Tim truly knows how to treat people worthy of honor.

A couple weeks later, Pelco hosted an event called a fire muster. A fire muster is a friendly competition between different fire departments. The one at Pelco lasted two days and featured a display of fire trucks from different eras. The festivities started with a parade of all the rigs. They continued with lots of competitions, fun games, and great food. That event was capped with a night of dancing, musical performances, and a special dinner, all taking place on Pelco's property.

I had heard that Ground Zero photographer Gary Suson would be present signing his book titled *Requiem*. I had to meet him! I didn't know much about him, and I wanted to learn more. After passing out flags to spectators at the parade and helping in the museum, I took off to find Gary. I bought a copy of his book and talked with him briefly. I told him briefly what had happened with me and my job. "About all I could do was pick up my phone and listen," I told him. "I gained some lifelong friends."

The wonderful photographer grabbed my hand and said, "You just made one more. It is so important to listen."

How true his statement was! By then, I really understood that simply listening is one of the most powerful steps in helping someone heal.

Looking through Gary's book was very emotional for me. By now, I'd come to know so many of the New York heroes that it was poignant to see in the book the faces of some I've come to know personally. I told Gary about this and mentioned names. One name was that of Battalion Chief Steve Zaderiko. I saw his picture in Gary's book a couple of times.

Later, at home, I looked through my pictures and papers from the last trip to the east coast. I found the note Chief Zaderiko wrote for me – to visit the exhibit of Gary Suson. Neally and I had tried our best to find that exhibit on our last day in New York, but somehow we had missed it. Now here I was, meeting the man behind the camera.

Gary spent nine months at Ground Zero. He suffered the same breathing problems many of the first responders and construction workers suffered. Today he remains busy creating plays and exhibits in honor of those lost on 9/11, keeping their memory alive. He donates much of what comes in from these efforts to 9/11-related charities.

A couple months later, I received an e-mail from Gary, notifying me of a book signing at the Clovis Fire Department Headquarters. I informed people at Pelco. I was one of several Pelco people who stopped by that book signing. I have realized that personal support of any effort to remember and honor the sacrifice of a hero's loved ones is another help in healing the heroes' hearts.

CHAPTER 25

US ARMY SPECIAL FORCES

Tom O'Neill had found a flag in the ruins of the World Trade Center. He had recovered it from the mud on one of the streets around Ground Zero. It had been buried in the dirt and debris and was very dirty. Tom took it home and washed it lovingly. The once-muddy flag flew proudly in the St. Patrick's Day Parade on Staten Island. Tom kept it in his headquarters for a time, and then he took it to his cabin in the Poconos.

When Tom's friend John and his son-in-law Paul Sweeney visited him in the Poconos, Tom showed them the flag. Paul was in the Army – Special Forces. He asked if he could borrow the flag and take it with him overseas. Tom could think of no more fitting place for the rescued flag than with the troops fighting the terrorism that had sought to destroy it. Paul eventually took the flag to both Afghanistan and Iraq.

On one of Paul's visits home, Tom called me and asked if I would contact the soldier. "I think you should talk to him," he said. "It would be good for him."

This was not the first time Tom had done something like this. Nor would it be the last. Tom has referred several people to me, telling them they needed to talk with me. Between Tom, Neil, and a few others who called often – and the people they were referring to me – I was beginning to feel a bit like "Dear Abby"… or "Delilah" from the soft rock stations.

I called Paul as Tom had asked and we talked for about thirty minutes. My heart was heavy as I listened to all that this young soldier had experienced. I ached for him just as I did for Neil and so many of the guys from New York. What could I say to someone like Paul, who was defending American freedoms, when I had not done anything remotely like what he was doing? What did I have to offer someone who put his life on the line regularly for others? Tom had sent me pictures of Paul and his unit. In one picture, the men of his unit were holding up the flag and a band of Kurdish soldiers was by their side. Paul told me he enjoyed seeing the world. He felt like he was doing something good for the people in the nations where he had been sent. Not only was he defending freedom for Americans, but he was helping people of other countries to gain their freedom. He believed this very deeply. He also said that he felt that God was with them.

When Paul came back from Afghanistan and Iraq in August of 2003, his commander sent him and his entire unit to meet Tom and give him back the flag he had recovered at Ground Zero. The unit was to meet him at Engine 167 Ladder 87 on Staten Island. The newspapers and the TV stations heard of the return of the symbol of American strength and pride, and they made the news public. As the day of the arrival of the soldiers drew near, the event had become so big that Tom was overwhelmed. "All I did was pull a flag out of the mud and clean it up, and now look what has become of it!"

What became of it was a major media event. A fire engine drove Paul's young children up and down the street. Cameras snapped photos and reporters carried the story. Several newspapers and the firehouse website printed the story, complete with pictures of Paul's whole unit with Tom and the flag. A solid bond was built between Paul Sweeney's unit and Engine 167 Ladder 87. Paul was made an honorary fire fighter.

When I saw the newspaper clippings Tom sent me and the websites, I smiled because I saw evidence of another strong bond. A bond between New York and California … between the heroes and those who simply wanted to help them heal. Tom was wearing a Pelco shirt.

CHAPTER 26

FIRE AND MILITARY BECOME ONE

September 11, 2003

As the second anniversary of the terrorist attacks approached, media coverage of the event again increased. On the eve of the anniversary, I made sure to send a message of greeting to all my New York friends. I think I will always remember the anniversary this way. It seemed some of the sadness had faded, so my message was brighter than the one the year before. The first anniversary felt like a day of extreme heaviness, anxiety, and sorrow. But the heroes who had been so devastated appeared to be slowly healing.

How would Neil do on this day? The fact that I was receiving regular messages from him gave me hope he would weather the two-year mark. When he is depressed, he doesn't write or send jokes. On the day of 9/11, I called him on his cell phone. He was walking from his mom's home to the firehouse around the block.

"I'm calling to check on you," I said.

"I knew you would," he responded. I asked him how he was doing.

"I woke up crying," he admitted.

All I could say was, "I'm sorry." I hoped I would say the right words. *At least he is going to the firehouse*, I thought. Maybe work would push the memories from his mind.

I think every anniversary will always touch each person differently. A letter from Gail Silke touched me. Here is a portion of what Gail wrote:

> *Of course everyone was crazy with September 11th. My father and sisters and brother and our spouses all went down to Ground Zero. The police picked us up at 5:00 am. What a day! The weather was the same as two years ago – a little eerie. After the ceremony, Goldman Sachs had purchased a boat for the NYPD and it was christened by Mayor Bloomberg – the name is "23 Heroes." It was beautiful! On our way home we stopped at my brother's truck and the bagpipers showed up. WOW! I cried more this day than the first anniversary. I guess the 1st anniversary I was in shock and now reality really kicked in.*

Once we got to my dad's house, which was around 4:00 pm, I ordered pizza and beers. Then finally went home to get the kids and go to 7 pm mass followed by a ceremony at the Cornerstone Memorial Park. Then home. Finally around 9:30 pm to bed. Well to say the least, the day was a tough one. Even though my brother died and it was the hardest day of our lives, we have met terrific people like you and Pelco. You guys are terrific!

Tell everyone we send our love. Look forward to meeting you all again.

In September, Paul's unit was deployed to Afghanistan again. A few weeks after he left, I got a nine a.m. call from Tom O'Neill: "Sue! I have to let you know. I just heard from my friend John Allardyce [Paul's father-in-law] right now. Sue, Paul is hurt! His unit was ambushed. Paul has been shot! I don't know if he is alive or not right now! John called me as soon as he heard and I'm calling you."

Hours later, Tom learned that Paul was in a hospital in Pakistan. He'd been shot in the head.

Around 5 p.m. I received a call from Tom's wife, Fran. She blurted out the news: "Sue! Paul is dead! I feel so bad! I'm calling because Tom is too upset. He can't talk right now." Fran was weeping terribly. I sank to my knees and prayed.

Neil Malone saw an article about Paul's death in the *New York Daily News* and e-mailed it to me. I saw a small article about it in our own Fresno newspaper. In our paper, however, all that was said was "Special Forces Staff Sergeant killed when unit was ambushed in Afghanistan." No name was given, but I knew it was Paul. What a connection across the country! Engine 167 Ladder 87, and especially Craig Chille, took up the responsibility of looking after Paul's family.

The process of returning a fallen soldier from overseas is lengthy. Paul's body went from Pakistan to Germany and then to the United States. Tom kept me informed about Paul's family and the arrangements for the funeral. The funeral saw a huge turnout of both military personnel and people from the New York City Fire Department. It took place a few days before Veteran's Day.

On Veteran's Day, Tom called me. "My friend John is really down about losing his son-in-law," he began. "This day, in particular, is really tough for him. A high school is doing a special tribute to Paul. Why don't you give John a call?" And he gave me his number.

"I already told him you'd call," he urged. "You can call around five p.m., your time. He said he'd be home around that time." I guess that settled it. I promised I'd call John.

At precisely five p.m., Pacific time, I dialed.

"Hello?"

"Hi! This is Sue Okenyi. I'm a friend of Tom's."

"Yes! He told me about you. What can I do for you?"

"Well, Tom has told me so much about Paul and I just wanted to call and ask you how you are doing."

We had a long conversation. John told me a lot about Paul, about his character and his personality. I asked John about his own military background. He had spent thirty years in the Navy, serving from Vietnam through Desert Storm. He told me of some of his experiences throughout the years. John and Tom have been lifelong friends from about the age of two. They grew up in the same projects. Family moves separated them and they met up again in the Navy. After a few years in the military, they were split up again, but were reunited several years ago and vowed to never lose track of each other ever again.

All I did was listen and ask a few questions, but it helped. People who are hurting need to know that others care about their pain. Those who have lost loved ones need to tell someone about that loved one. My call gave John the chance to proudly proclaim, "Paul died doing what he felt was right – fighting for our country and for freedom everywhere. I wish I could take up where he left off."

John could not take up where his son-in-law left off. But in a way, his friend Tom O'Neill had been doing the same kind of fighting. Tom was not still fighting for his country abroad, but until the injuries he suffered at Ground Zero forced him to retire, he and other first responders risked their lives every day so people at home could enjoy the freedom Paul died for. One day I was on the phone with Tom when he said abruptly, "Sue, can you hear this?" He had the television on while we were talking.

"Wait, I'll turn up the volume on the TV," he cried. "A ferry just crashed!" The news was reporting that just seven minutes earlier, a Staten Island ferry had crashed. As Tom watched the coverage, he remembered, "Sue, that ferry is the very one you were on when you came to visit! Oh, this is bad!"

I heard about the crash again the next day. Neil called. "Sue, I just want you to know," he began, "I was there."

"Where?" I asked.

"I was in Staten Island yesterday," he explained. "My company was called to the scene. It was bad! There were body parts; it was ugly."

I was humbled to realize that people like Neil face horror and panic regularly. They feel the shock, the revulsion, the sadness. Then they pick up the pieces. And they go back to work the next day and do it all over again.

"Guess who I saw there?" Neil continued. "I saw Sal, the one I told my story to, the one who was in the stairwell." Sal had been in the stairwell of the World Trade Center helping an elderly woman; he was one of six fire fighters to make it out alive. Neil had told him about his encounter with the Arab boy. He knew that Sal lived on Staten Island. He was off duty, but when he heard about the crash, he had suited up and come to help. Neil was concerned for him. "I went up to him," he said, "and told him, 'It's bad; you might not want to go in there.' I felt it was kind of like 9/11 – that gruesome.

"And that wasn't all that happened yesterday! I had gotten a ginger ale and was walking back to the firehouse when I saw something fly through the air. I knew right away the dark object was a person. A guy on a bike had been hit by a vehicle in a hit and run!"

I had a hard enough time imagining someone still so devastated by the horrors of the terrorist attacks having to deal with the deaths on the ferry. But another violent incident on the same day ... and right in front of him.

Neil described the scene: "The guy was thrown about thirty feet! I ran over to him. He was bad! I ran back to the firehouse to alert the guys, and then ran back to the guy."

All this in a day's work. How do people go home and sort that kind of stuff out and still say they love their job? Since meeting and corresponding with so many police and firemen, I have a tremendous appreciation for them and the services they perform.

The second anniversary was barely over before the holidays were upon us. Neil called me one day while he was decorating his house. He told me it had been snowing and the scene was beautiful. He was playing Christmas music. Over the phone, he sang "Oh Holy Night," impersonating Elmer Fudd through the whole song. He seemed in good spirits, relaxed, and happy. This was a big change from the year before, and I prayed it would continue.

CHAPTER 27

THE BLAME GAME

The year 2004 brought the 9/11 Commission. Once again, my New York friends had virtually no choice but to hear incessant coverage of the 9/11 tragedy. With the reports of the hearings, news programs were airing pictures from that day and playing audio. The officers in charge from the different agencies were being grilled. All the talk not only kept wounds open, but inflicted new ones.

Members of the police and fire departments and the Port Authority were especially angered by an accusation from John Lehman that placed blame on the first responders. Dan D'Allara was in the audience when Lehman called the response of the rescuers "scandalous." Sitting four rows from the front, he seethed with indignation. After the hearing, as Lehman hurried out of the room, Dan stood and yelled at him. "I didn't mean to," he said later, "but I told him off. Not my style!" But he did it anyway.

The next day, when the newspapers reported Lehman's apology, the congressman used the exact phrase Dan had shouted at him: "It was a poor choice of words."

Dan D'Allara was not the only one who was upset by the hearings. When Neil called me about them, he was so filled with rage he couldn't speak. All he could manage to say was "I'm listening to the 9/11 Commission. They're blaming us!" He hung up three times, each time I would call him back, before he could compose himself enough to talk about what was being said. "They blame us!" he cried in disbelief. "They say we are a bunch of worthless Boy Scouts!"

What a slap in the face of those who gave so much for so many that awful day and time. I was angry, too. How could anyone disparage the brave people who died and those who risked death to save others? How could they say they were not up to the task? Nothing could be further from the truth.

I listened a little more as Neil vented his frustration and hurt. Finally, I got him to joke a bit. This was something that was becoming habit – trying to bring a laugh in the midst of a painful conversation.

I knew Neil wasn't the only one who was distressed and angry. That night, I sent a general message to all my New York friends:

I am hoping all is well with everyone. Out here on the west coast our thoughts and prayers are with you all as the 9/11 Commission continues. All members of the uniformed services did the very best anyone could do.
Take care and God Bless.

Tony Whitaker responded to my e-mail:

The 9/11 Commission hearings have caused a lot of negative reaction in the police and fire communities – with the commission playing the blame game. The sentiment here is that the commission has missed the point, which is: the bad guys are the terrorists. As for me, I've received some telephone and e-mail from around the country asking why I was not called to testify. Given the atmosphere of the "Blame Game," I'm better off on the sidelines.

The feelings of so many about the 9/11 Commission – first responders and ordinary citizens – were summed up in an item that appeared on the cover of the *New York Post* soon after the commission ended its hearings. It was a picture of a fire fighter at Ground Zero with the caption "INSULT. Memo to 9/11 Commission: This man is a New York HERO. He is not a 'Boy Scout!'" That said it as well as anything could.

At one point in the 9/11 Commission hearings, certain details were revealed regarding warnings of a terrorist attack prior to the actual event. This devastated Neil. The date of August 6, 2001, came up. This was the day Neil was electrocuted responding to the call on the subway – the day after he met the little Moroccan boy on the ambulance, the little boy who asked him if he was going to work on 9-11.

Although difficult, Neil got through that incident. I felt he was truly healing. Painful incidents would come up and he'd call me or he'd catch me online and send me instant messages. On the day of the 9/11 anniversary in 2004 he actually was able to joke a bit.

He was doing so well that he even entertained the thought of coming with some of his friends to California. However, their plans fell through. "If we ever come," he warned me, "we're not going to tell you ahead of time. If we come, we want no fanfare. We don't want anyone to make a big deal out of it. We'll just slip in and out." I was disappointed that he wasn't coming, but I was happy that he seemed to be doing so much better.

Things seemed to be better for many of the New York heroes. One example is the story of Andy Isolano. Just weeks prior to 9/11, he underwent a divorce. When the tragedy occurred, he kept himself busy, volunteering to work Ground Zero whenever he could. On November 12, 2001, he was "ordered off the pile and went sick." He had developed breathing problems from working Ground Zero, and they had taken a heavy toll on his health. He was prescribed many different asthma medications, but they barely helped him to breathe. He was out of the FDNY for good.

On December 8, 2001, Andy attended Pelco's memorial event. On that trip, he made a very special friend and their relationship blossomed into love. Andy made the choice to leave New York and move to California. Around the same time, he underwent a special treatment program at the New York Detoxification Project. This organization, co-founded by Tom Cruise, was helping people who had suffered the effects of breathing in deadly toxins at Ground Zero. Although set up to help the first responders, the program was extended to absolutely anyone who lived or worked in the area during the time of the attacks and the rescue and recovery efforts. It involves taking vitamins, running on a treadmill or riding a stationary bike, and sitting in a sauna. The patients sweat out the toxins. It has proven to be very effective. For Andy, it restored a good part of his quality of life.

For Neil, it looked as though the quality of life was also coming back. At Thanksgiving 2004, he sent me a wonderful e-card (see next page). In that card, Neil said three times that he was thankful. He admitted in no uncertain terms that he owed his life to the thin but strong thread of friendship between us. This was touching beyond words; it made me cry. I don't think I'll ever fully understand how just listening, caring, and trying to be encouraging could be so important. However it works, I too was glad that I could be a friend. Like Neil, I was also very thankful.

Thanksgiving 2004

"Thank you" is a small thing to say to someone who is such a big part of my life. But I hope you know how much your friendship means to me today and always.

Have a Very Happy Thanksgiving

Dear Sue,
What can I say? I'm very thankful for your friendship! I have alot to be thankful for! If it weren't for you and, your many prayers, you know I wouldn't be here today! Wishing you and your family a very Happy Thanksgiving!!!!!!!!
Love Always
Me :)

CHAPTER 28

NEW YORK DETOX

Early 2005, Andy Isolano was getting settled into his new home in California. He had been promising me he'd get together with me to talk about the book I was writing about the 9/11 heroes, but nothing had worked out until now. Finally he was able to meet and we had a wonderful lunch together. The meal took much longer than I expected. Andy explained much of his story and touched on the incredible friendships he had gained. I asked him to tell me about the New York Rescue Workers Detoxification Project.

He did better than explain the project to me. He put me in touch with Jim Woodworth, co-executive director of the program. Eventually, we all met in California: Andy, Jim, and a retired FDNY fire fighter named Joe Higgins.

Joe had known almost all the guys killed on 9/11/01. He had trained most of them. Joe is a Marine (he refuses to say ex-Marine). He is heavily into physical fitness. He too suffered breathing problems from working at Ground Zero and underwent the NY Detox Program. He now spends his time promoting the program and running a gym for underprivileged kids.

Pelco Vice President Tim Glines talked with Andy, Jim, and Joe for about three hours. Then we all walked to the site of the museum and the memorial. When we reached the monument, Joe leaned over toward the plaque. "I just have to touch it!" he said, his voice thick with emotion. Tim reached into his pocket and brought out one of Pelco's Hero Medals – the medal that was given to all the guys who came from New York in December 2001. He placed it around Joe's neck and said "Welcome home, brother, to your second home." Then Tim turned to Jim Woodworth and brought another medal out of his pocket. "This is for you for all you do trying to help the guys," he explained.

When we entered the museum, the guys were overcome with remembering that awful day and its aftermath. We spent about half an hour in the museum and then it was time for lunch. They ate fast! Fire fighters learn to eat quickly. In the firehouse, they don't know how much time they will have before needing to go out on a call, and they might not get back in time to finish dinner.

Before Jim and Joe caught their plane, we were all able to meet briefly with Mr. McDonald. Mr. McDonald knew Andy because he had come often and had made friends with many Pelco people. He took the opportunity to tease him: "So, Andy, when are you moving to California?"

Andy replied, "I'm already out here!"

"What?" Mr. McDonald said in mock shock. "You mean you're already here and you haven't come to see me? I saw you more when you lived in New York!" It was a great exchange, and Andy promised to visit him.

I have kept contact with Andy and with Jim Woodworth from the Detox Project. I have reviewed what they do and talked to several who have gone through the program and others who truly want to give it a try. I have found the program to be highly regarded by many in both the police and fire departments. Jim has expressed to me that if a rescue worker spent even just two hours at Ground Zero, that, coupled with years of exposure to toxins, would be enough to qualify him to go through the program free of charge.

CHAPTER 29

COMING FULL CIRCLE

On Thursday, just before Easter 2005, I was surprised by a phone call from Neil.

"Sue, don't pray for me anymore!" he began.

Oh no, I thought. *What's happening with him?* But Neil was quick to continue: "Don't pray for *me*. I want you to pray for a friend of mine. He tried to commit suicide yesterday!"

I was taken aback. *Tried* to commit suicide. "Is he okay now?" I wondered aloud.

Neil thought he was. The man is a retired fire fighter, and Neil sought to understand the reason he would do the very thing Neil himself had wanted to do barely three years earlier. "I know he spent time at Ground Zero," he reasoned. "I know he lost friends that day, but he retired in the 80s and went into another line of work."

Then Neil got to the heart of what was really bothering him about the incident. "The weird thing about this," he said, "was it was on a train track!"

Uh-oh, I thought. For Neil, train tracks bring up memories of his electrocution. Two months earlier, he had been called to another emergency on a train track. In that incident, as with his, the power had not been turned off. A woman had been decapitated. Neil froze.

This time, the scene was equally frightening. "We were called out to a civilian on the tracks," he explained. "When we got there, we had no idea if the person was injured, dead, or what. It wasn't the subway. It was an above-ground train. You know the track you see in the beginning of the show 'Blind Justice'? That was it! The officer in charge sent me to go up and check on the person.

"When I reached the platform, I saw this guy on the tracks. He had lain down across the tracks and waited for the train. But someone saw him and the train stopped ten inches from his head! He was alive. I thought he looked familiar. I jumped down onto the tracks. Then I recognized him! It was a guy named John. It was weird with it being train tracks, and I was electrocuted on the subway. No one else recognized him.

"I told him I was in the same place myself about four years ago but a friend in California and her friends prayed me through. It's Easter week, I told him. This is when we recognize what Jesus Christ did for us, so let's go home and have a new life. John got up and I told the rest of the guys 'he's a fire fighter.'"

I breathed a sigh of relief. "I'm glad he's all right!" I said sincerely. "I will pray for him. I'll pray for the two of you."

"No," Neil interrupted. "I want all the prayers, all the energy to go to John. You've prayed for me enough."

Of course there is enough "energy" in even a brief prayer to cover both men. But I assured Neil I would pray for the man he rescued. I marveled at what had just taken place. Neil was encouraging someone else. For so long, he was in need of support from others, and now he was the one reaching out with strength to another desperately hurting man. Who better to understand what John was going through? Who better to lift him up? The deeply wounded Neil had received encouragement and help, and now he was giving encouragement and help to someone else. I wrote a friend who had helped me pray for Neil: "What starts with one is passed on."

About one month prior to the 9/11 anniversary, I spoke with Neil again. "Any chance you and your friends will come out to California for the 9/11 memorial this year?" I asked.

"No," Neil answered quite quickly! "No, no plans to come out there." I don't quite remember the rest of the conversation, but I became a little concerned when phone calls, e-mails, and instant messages from Neil slowed to a halt. I reminded myself of the progress he'd made and told myself that he was probably just really busy. Nevertheless, worry for him still nagged at my heart.

Pushing the worry from my mind, I busied myself preparing for the observance of the 9/11 anniversary that would take place at Pelco. I was to be a "roving reporter," asking questions of people in attendance for our local media company. I also volunteered to cover the museum for part of the time. Few people know the exhibits as well as I do.

Early in the afternoon on September 8, I received a call from Dora Linares. "Have you heard from Neil?" she asked.

I hadn't heard much from him lately.

"Well I have!" she said. "He said he sent me a package. And he said he sent one to you, too!"

"Really?" I was intrigued. What would Neil be sending to the two of us? Before I could think much about it, a call came in from Neil on his cell phone: "Sue! Have you received a package from me?"

This was getting even more interesting. Why all the excitement and suddenness about a package from New York? "No," I said. I had received nothing.

"Well, I sent you something," he insisted. "It's coming FedEx. I told them it had to be there by 2:00 because you go home early. I'm going to hang up so I can call FedEx and trace the package. I'll call you back."

Now I was really eager to get this mysterious gift. I stayed close to my desk, hoping our Receiving Department would notify me of a delivery. Precisely at two p.m., I received a call from the receptionist in our lobby, asking me to come and sign for a package.

As I walked into the lobby, I was so lost in anticipation and puzzlement that I didn't notice how many people were standing there, doing nothing. Even with all the people, I didn't see anyone from FedEx. Then, I heard a voice, familiar but out of place: "So do I get a hug?" There in front of me, with a "gotcha" grin all over his face, was Neil Malone! He had done just what he promised: come without notice or fanfare. He was actually there!

Neil had brought with him Eileen Gregan from FDNY Battalion 35; Harry Gillen, FDNY retired from Ladder 131; and John Dillon, a former FDNY battalion chief, now retired. I had not met John before, and when I shook his hand, his first words to me were: "You said 'wow' five times!" I suppose I did. I was still in shock I couldn't believe they actually came and surprised me!

"I almost blew it yesterday on the phone," Neil said with a laugh.

If he did, I hadn't caught it. This "package" was a complete and unexpected surprise! For the record, Neil also brought cannoli for Dora and Italian cookies for me. He did bring actual gifts – personally delivered!

The four visitors would be in California for five days, and Neil's friend Buddy would join them a little later. My mind raced with ideas of how to make their stay special. I could not take off work completely because a co-worker was off and I was in charge of the Literature Department in his absence. But my managers were very understanding; they gave me flexibility so I could entertain my guests.

The first evening, I picked them up at their hotel and we all went to dinner. Neil gave me the biggest hug! I cracked up listening to the firemen tease each other. Harry and John joked about their ages. John explained what was on the menu for the Last Supper and Harry came back with, "I wouldn't know! I wasn't there!" They laughed that, with the resources they have now, they would have put out the burning bush Moses encountered.

We were having so much fun, I almost forgot how difficult returning to California must be for Neil. He told me he slept only a couple hours the previous night in anticipation of the trip. This was a big step for him to make, and it signaled healing.

The next day, our guests became typical tourists; they went to our beautiful Yosemite National Park. In the evening, my husband, Sam, and I were on our way to their hotel to take them to dinner. Before we got there, Neil called my cell phone. "Listen," he said, "don't come. I've got a splitting headache and Eileen is snoring. The other guys aren't dressed to go anywhere."

"We're just around the block," I replied. My husband wanted to at least stop by and see how they were doing.

"Whatever you think," Neil said with resignation.

It took a while, but eventually everyone dressed and met us for dinner. Sam and John became instant friends. It seemed neither one stopped talking the whole night! Wanting to treat them to a memorable evening, we took them to a wonderful restaurant famous for its atmosphere, live jazz, and prime rib. This night, however, there was no jazz. And the cook was inexplicably out of prime rib. The night was certainly memorable! In spite of the surprises, everyone had a great time.

Back at the hotel, Neil walked my husband and me to the car. He turned to talk very seriously with Sam. "I want to apologize to you if I have taken your wife away from the family at all these past four years," he began. "I want you to know that she has been my lifeline."

Neil went on to explain portions of his story to Sam, even though I had told Sam all about his struggles. Sam listened and encouraged him; then the two men embraced. I was so glad for that conversation. I know that my friendship with Neil is very unconventional. Many people may not understand such a deep bond that is in no way romantic. Sam understands. He watched Neil's story unfold just as I did, little by little. He heard every detail the same days I did. He saw me weep and pray over my friend, and he understands our relationship. Sam believes, as I do, that reaching out to a hurting person is what God calls us to do.

On the weekend, some of our guests wanted to go to church. Sam and I agreed to go to Mass with them, but Neil said he wasn't going. "I haven't been in a church for thirty years," he explained.

I told him I kind of hoped he would visit my church. "Some of your fans are there," I prodded. "People who have prayed for you."

"Don't hold your breath," was his answer.

I didn't hold my breath, but Neil relented a little. When we got to the church for Mass, he was there!

That evening, Pelco held a rehearsal for the 9/11 memorial ceremony that was to take place the following morning. After the rehearsal, a dinner was to be served. I laughed when I saw that the menu was prime rib.

At the rehearsal, I told Casey Clark about the surprise visit from the five New Yorkers. Casey dug into his pocket and handed me tickets for the Field of Wishes Baseball game – a yearly friendly competition between Fresno Police and Fresno Fire. Proceeds go to the Make-A-Wish Foundation. "Bring them to the game," Casey said. Like so many of us, Casey thinks of the New York rescuers as heroes. He wants to do whatever is in his power to honor them.

The dinner turned out to be an honor for them, too. I was asked to announce their presence. I hesitated because Neil had seemed very nervous since he arrived for the meal. But I was also proud to introduce my friends to the crowd. As I did, I heard Neil say quietly, "I shouldn't have come." My heart sank. I understood how difficult this was for him. The memories he came here to face were beyond painful. I knew he wanted to just slip in and slip out – no big deal. But that wasn't going to happen.

After dinner, our friends did not want the night to end. They asked us to go with them to the hotel bar to visit further. Sitting at a bar was a little uncomfortable for Sam and me, but we wanted to be with our friends. While there, we noticed a tall, handsome military man at the front desk, checking in with his wife. Neil invited them – Robi and Julie – to join us. He wanted to do something to honor Robi for his military service. We all hit it off and had a great time together.

In the course of the conversation, Neil began to tell Julie a bit of why he came to California. "Something very terrible almost happened four years ago here," he told her. "I came to face that. For the last four years, this woman has been my lifeline."

Julie seemed to understand.

"She's writing a book," Neil went on. Looking at me, he said, "Tell her what it's about."

"It's about him," I said with a smile.

As Neil continued to reveal parts of his story, I could see him struggling. But he needed to talk. This was why he had come. He had made the trip to California to face the darkest part of his story and overcome its hold on him. Every time he shared out loud what he had almost done, the power of the memory weakened. Still, it was hard.

Probably the most difficult for him would be the memorial observance the next day. That night, I slept for maybe an hour. I prayed for Neil continually, prayed that the events surrounding the ceremony would bring further healing.

The morning of September 11th, my family went to the breakfast Pelco served for the firemen, the police, and the military. We found Neil very stressed. He said he had not slept all night. I caught up with him in a private moment, between some buildings.

"Neil," I ordered, "give me your hand." He did.

"Bow your head," I instructed. He did.

I pulled in close and prayed in his ear: "Dear Heavenly Father. Thank you for my friend and all You've done for him these last few years. He has come a long way in his healing. More work remains. Please be with him right now. Cover him with your peace and give him strength in this moment. In Jesus' name, Amen."

Neil gave me a quick "Thank you!" as he fought back tears. He handed me a pack of tissues. "Hold these for me," he said.

I was supposed to be a roving reporter during the ceremony. But I was too emotional to talk with crowds of people that way. My supervisors understood, and they excused me from that responsibility.

The ceremony started with the audio of the first portion of the dispatch tapes from the attacks of 9/11/01. It was unbearable for me to listen, but for my friends, it must have been worse. The tapes took them back to that horrible day. I was standing behind them to be as close as possible, giving support with my presence. After the tapes, Eileen Gregan and Harry Gillen walked up to the monument and placed on it the wreath their little group had brought.

A procession followed: highway patrol cars and a vintage fire truck bearing the members of the local company along with Billy Hayes from the FDNY. Wreaths representing the different agencies and the military were presented, and flags were presented to Billy Hayes and PAPD Chief Anthony Whitaker. The flag was lowered to half staff while *Taps* was played by two buglers echoing back and forth – one on the ground and one on the roof of Pelco's Building Three. The ceremony ended with a 21-gun salute.

When the solemn, gripping ceremony ended, Neil stood stiffly, unable to move, overcome with emotion. I touched his arm to let him know I was there but I didn't want to impose on his thoughts. Someone came up to speak to me, and when I turned back around, Neil was nowhere in sight! But Sam had seen him leave. "He went for a walk. He's okay," he assured me. "Robi is with him."

Robi, the soldier he barely knew, was walking silently beside him, lending him his strength. They were comrades, brothers who shared a common tragedy, a common fear, a common pain. They did not need to speak.

After a while, Neil was back in the main area and we all went to the museum together. Buddy noticed one of the pictures taken of the Ground Zero area. He pointed out a flag hanging from a window. He told me he had put that flag there. Harry saw a picture of the four of them minus John from the December 8, 2001, ceremony at Pelco. Buddy commented, "I was fatter then."

"Then?" Harry quipped.

Then Buddy pointed out a female fire fighter in a drawing of an active fire scene. "That's Eileen," he suggested. "She posed for that."

Harry said, "It's not a very good picture of her."

Buddy had brought some pictures for Mr. McDonald – large prints of laser etchings from the Brooklyn Wall of Remembrance on Coney Island. Each picture from the wall depicts one of the fallen fire fighters or police officers from Brooklyn. Today they are framed and hang in the stairwell leading up to Mr. McDonald's office.

At the Field of Wishes softball game that evening, Billy Hayes, who is FDNY and came from New York, was playing on the fire fighters' team. We had a great time cheering him on. John yelled comments to Billy that I was told were heard on the field!

My husband promised them an "authentic Italian dinner" after the game. We laughed that Sam, a Nigerian-born citizen who had not had anything Italian in his life before coming to the United States, was taking a New Yorker who was born and raised Italian out for Italian food.

We squeezed so much into the few days of that surprise visit. A tour of Pelco, sightseeing in central California, lots of visiting and eating. I had to make sure Neil met certain people he had become familiar with over the phone. Neil honored my daughter's request to speak to her class.

I think we sent them off happy for having come. For Neil, however, "happy" might not be the right word. I know his feelings were mixed. It wasn't easy for him to come and face this place again. But he did it. He came full circle. He will continue moving forward, not backward. The deep wounds are being closed. The scars will always be there, but scars only show us where we've been … and remind us that we are no longer there. The hero's heart is healing.

CHAPTER 30

IN THEIR OWN WORDS

"At the time I was still working and looking for my son Gary who was lost in Tower 1. I went to California to take a break from Ground Zero. I was thankful that people 3,000 miles away reached out to comfort and acknowledge New Yorkers. It was one of the warmest welcomes I have ever received. When returning from the Korean War in 1953, there was nothing. I want to thank each and every one of you wonderful people for that Memorial Day. I miss my son Gary each and every day."

Paul E. Geidel
FDNY – retired

"The best healing can come from being surrounded by friends and those who truly care about your well-being. I was taken aback by the invitation to come to California and spend a few days with people that wanted to experience our pain, our broken hearts, and our souls.

"Stepping off the plane was a surreal moment in my life. I saw a line of law enforcement on the runway, a marching band and so many people that were unknown to me. But they emanated a heartfelt warmth and cheer that caused my heart to feel appreciation and understanding for what we had been through. A hero's welcome had to come 3,000 miles away from home. This made me fall instantly enamored with the good people of Clovis, Fresno and the great state of California. Thanks could never measure my feeling for all."

Lt. Claudio Fernandez
NYPD Highway Patrol

"I was one of the fortunate employees that got to be a driver that weekend of 12/08/01. I got to witness firsthand the pain they were still feeling. To see them go from a solemn, sad mood to a somewhat jovial, happier mood.

By the time they left that Sunday morning, every one of them was glad they had come and so were we. Every time since then that some of them would come for an event such as the Clovis Rodeo Parade, I was blessed to be a driver. I feel honored to be a part of all of this."

Neadly Foster
Pelco – Manufacturing Department

"My involvement came from flying Gloria Hatcher – The Brownie Lady – and her friend Diane to Fresno in order to see Sue at Pelco. We had an incredible, hospitable tour of Pelco and of the California Memorial. It truly was a blessing meeting Sue as well as a few other folks, including Mr. McDonald. As a fire fighter for over thirty years, I was very moved by everyone's love and commitment to honor the tragic loss to our profession as well as police, Port Authority personnel, and the men and women of the aircraft involved. Thank you all, from the bottom of my heart. May God bless you all."

Barry Hasterok
Orange County Fire Authority

"In those dark days after 9/11, I witnessed the greatness of this country in a manner I never imagined.

"The terrorist attacks happened during my family's vacation to Ohio. The airline cancelled our flights back to Fresno … and with problems at the airports and fears of terrorists still lurking about – my wife and I decided to drive our family back to California from Ohio. I kept notes and we took snapshots along the way. Our long journey revealed the American spirit … still very much alive.

"From the heartland to the Central Valley, we saw Old Glory waving proudly. A car show in Illinois celebrated the Corvette's speed and style, but it quickly turned patriotic with flags flying on every car.

"The high desert of Arizona, where long ago a meteorite carved out a massive crater, included shades of red, white, and blue.

"Trucks, RV's, and campers from Ohio to California also packed the Stars and Stripes.

"Messages of faith and solidarity on billboards and signs of all sizes dotted the landscape.

"Everywhere we stopped, TV's and radios were always on, providing the latest information for those who could stop and watch … and then carry on with their business or travel.

"At a truck stop in a desolate part of New Mexico, we found a donation jar for victims of the attacks and their families – Americans doing whatever they can to help each other.

"We met a woman named Pia who worked at a motel in Barstow. She told us about other families she met in recent days – forced to drive to weddings and funerals instead of flying. Various state license plates in parking lots confirmed the travel.

"With our two little boys and the future in our backseat … we drove through a spectacular country – made great by its people and their pride and passion.

"Months later, on a beautiful December Day in Clovis, I anchored live coverage on ABC-30 of the Dedication of The California Memorial at Pelco. We all thought and prayed for those who sacrificed. I gave thanks for my family's safety on our cross-country trip and for those everyday people who make this country great."

Warren Armstrong
News Anchor, KFSN-TV ABC-30

This next gentleman did not come to California and does not speak of the Memorial. He attended the Dedication Ceremony in Orangeburg and became a friend because of that. He is in the pictures of that event – a big man with an awesome jacket filled with patches. He is a comic/novelty shop owner. Since 9/11 he and his family, along with a group of volunteers, have been cooking meals for firehouses:

"We have now completed 133 firehouse dinners since 9/11. The Ramos Family embarked on this mission of mercy to honor our heroes. We have now fed over 3,000 fire fighters on this mission. The Ramos girls, my wife Yvette, my three daughters Jizelle, Jeanette, and Sharon have been a major part of this mission. The volunteers are also great assets to this endeavor of love."

Jose Ramos
Bronx, NY

"I remember turning the TV on at five a.m. As I was getting ready for work, the news was on, as normal. Then, from the corner of my eye, I saw an airplane hit a building not knowing it was one of the towers. I thought they were showing scenes from an upcoming movie. Then a special bulletin was flashing on the screen and the second plane hit. I just sat on the bed and started to cry. It was unreal! New York was under attack. As the morning went on, things got worse. My oldest sister was returning home from Chicago that morning. We had not heard from her. Frantically, we waited. All planes had been grounded, four hijacked. Was she on one of them? After six hours, she called to say she was okay and she and other ladies would be driving home the next day if it was safe to do so. With God's blessing, the ladies arrived home safely.

"I was one of the drivers for the California Memorial. As a driver, I was responsible for taking and picking up any of the New York visitors from place to place, no matter what time it was. Our concern was that they have a good time. I met lots of neat people. I listened to a lot of sad, heartbreaking stories with which I cried right along with them. Boy, those New Yorkers can drink! I don't blame them. If I was mourning my friends, fellow officers, fire fighters, and relatives, I might do the same thing. But no matter how intoxicated those guys got, not once did they disrespect the women drivers. I take my hat off to them. I made lots of friends those days and will always hold the memories dear to my heart."

Dora Linares
Pelco - a receptionist at the time
She now works in National Accounts

"I will never forget looking on the faces of all the firemen and also watching from a distance as they went up to the Memorial itself. I think that that is an image I will never forget. Also, I will never forget the message Chuck Yeager gave. It was a message only he could give because he had been through wars. He had seen friends die. You saw WWII the last time when we were attacked. And then you know talking to the next generation some fifty odd years later, sixty odd years later really. That was really memorable to me. Also, what was most memorable to me was the look in David McDonald's eye. This really touched this man deeply. He wanted to do something significant to show the fire fighters, police, and Port Authority what they meant to the entire country.

Alan Autry
Mayor of Fresno and Master of Ceremonies

PICTURES

Flag presentation at Engine 167 Ladder 87.

At Tom and Fran's House: Patty Duffy, Neadly Foster, Fran O'Neill, Sue Okenyi, and Eric Duffy (seated)

Memorial at Our Lady of Perpetual Help – Staten Island. Many prayer cards and pictures in memory of the lost.

SSS Paul Sweeney and his command unit in Iraq. Paul has his back turned.

Staten Island Dispatch.

Tom O'Neill being awarded a plaque.

Diane Westlake, Gloria Hatcher ("The Brownie Lady"), Pelco Sr. Vice President Tim Glines, Orange County Fire Authority Engineer Barry Hasterok, Orange County Fire Authority Captain Kirk Wells.

Diane Westlake, Kacey Coulter, Sue Okenyi and Gloria Hatcher at Pelco

Pelco CEO Dave McDonald with Gloria Hatcher.

9/11/05 – (l to r) Retired Battalion Chief John Dillon, fire fighter Eileen Gregan (she was a driver for John at one time in the department), Neil Malone, retired fire fighter Harry Gillen and retired fire fighter Roman Ducalo.

Sign held by crowd along St. Patrick's Day parade route.

Mr. McDonald at St. Patrick's Day Reunion party in New York.

California Highway Patrol contingent at St. Patrick's Day parade.

The Dodrill family at the St. Patrick's Day parade.

343 Flags held by 343 FDNY members.

FDNY on the sidelines watching the parade.

Los Angeles County Fire Department.

Sue Okenyi with two FDNY fire fighters in front of the Milford Plaza Hotel.

NYPD Ride Along – Valerie Franco, Dora Linares and Sue Okenyi.

Tall Bagpipers and Sue Okenyi.

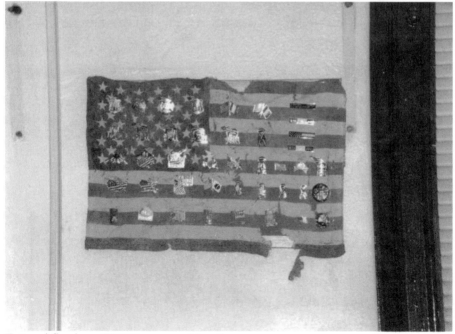

Tattered flag in an FDNY command location.

Valerie Franco and Sue Okenyi with the gentlemen of Hell's Kitchen.

Parade onlookers and an interesting "Irishman."

Paul Mains, married to Andrea Mains who worked for Pelco, at the St. Patrick's Day parade.

Cartoon in an FDNY location.

Words Cannot Express

Clovis fire fighter Tom Zinn dances with his daughter as bagpipers play at Orangeburg Dedication.

Wreaths prepared for the Orangeburg Dedication.

The Gerbasis and Sue Okenyi at the Orangeburg Dedication.

Roman Ducalo, Eileen Gregan, Sue Okenyi, Neil Malone, Harry Gillen.

Fresno entertainer Rhonda Grove dressed as Mae West at the Orangeburg Dedication.

Picture of fallen fire fighter Joseph Agnello on his empty chair. He had just been promoted to the title of Lieutenant, effective as of 9/11/2001.

Fresno mayor Alan Autry.

Fire Police Captain Kenneth O'Leary of the Sloatsburg Volunteer Fire Department.

Fire helmet from the Tappan Fire Department. Both the Sloatsburg and Tappan fire departments are near to Orangeburg, New York.

Airman Robi Yucas and Neil Malone.

Neil Malone with my husband Samuel Okenyi.

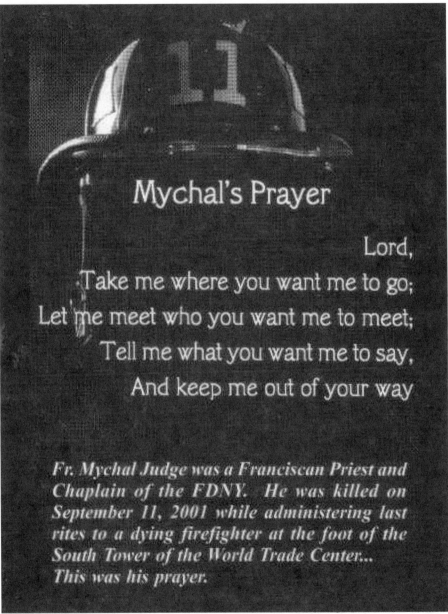

Mychal's Prayer.

Fire Department, City of New York
Memorial Day, October 12th, 2002

The program from the IAFF Memorial at Madison Square Garden – October 2002.

Eric and Patty Duffy (far left); Dan D'Allara, Neadly Foster, Gail Silke and Letitia Driscoll seated on the opposite side of the table. Sue Okenyi with Neil Malone, front.

Arriving at Marine Company One with Tim Keenan, Patrick Burns and Kevin Michaels from Ladder 123.

Gail Silke, Eric Duffy, Dan D'Allara, Neadly Foster, Letitia Driscoll and Sue Okenyi at Marine Company One.

Dinner with Engine 234 Ladder 123.

Gail Silke, Eric Duffy, Dan D'Allara, Kevin Bryant, Letitia Driscoll and Sue Okenyi.

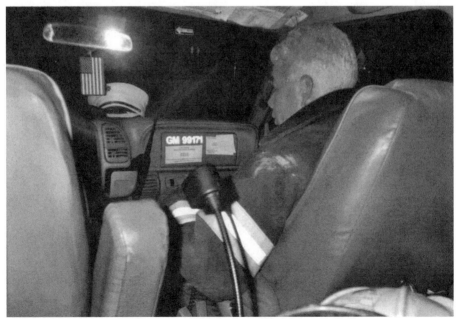

On a call with Ladder 123 riding with Battalion Chief Steve Zaderiko.

On the scene of a call.

Tim Keenan, Pat Burns and Kevin Michaels of Ladder 123.

Fire fighter Tim Keenan training men how to break down a door at Ladder 123.

Neadly Foster

Antique fire truck with fire fighter and Pelco VP, Tim Glines (standing).

Andy Isolano at the California Memorial.

The crowd at the California Memorial – December 8, 2001.

403 empty chairs symbolizing the Fallen Heroes of 9/11.

New York guests at the California Memorial.

General Chuck Yeager signing autographs for New York's Finest.

Chief Anthony Whitaker, Julie Debenedetto and PAPD Officer Michael Megna.

Monument at night.

Retired FDNY member Harry Gillen signs a flag for a little girl.

Harry Gillen, Eileen Gregan, Neil Malone, Roman Ducalo at the
December 8, 2001 Ceremony.

Soma Balber with General Chuck Yeager.

Barry McGuire, New York Opera baritone Richard Woods, Randy Deaver, Pelco Vice President Peter DalPezzo.

The Memorial Monument adorned with pictures and prayer cards of fallen heroes placed by living heroes.

The Memorial Plaque.

PAPD Deputy Chief Anthony Whitaker honored.

Memorial Plaque with flowers.

APPENDICES

NEIL MALONE

For decades Neil Malone has done all he can to save lives – on and off duty. He is one that will do all he can to help in any situation that arises whether it is a part of his job or not. When it comes to "flight or fight"…he fights. Some of these incidents are documented in these pages.

In the first two pictures, Neil with EMS partner Mike Hansen, help a rookie cop chase down a group of gun-toting robbers in their ambulance. The cop was standing on the sidewalk issuing a traffic violation when someone started yelling about some guys getting away. Neil and Mike told the cop to get in the ambulance and they chased down the perps – partly by ambulance, partly on foot. At one point during the chase Neil was able to subdue one of the perps by chasing him into a pizzeria. With his flashlight drawn as a weapon Neil told him to get down on his knees and then to lie on his belly. The officer was then able to arrest the suspect.

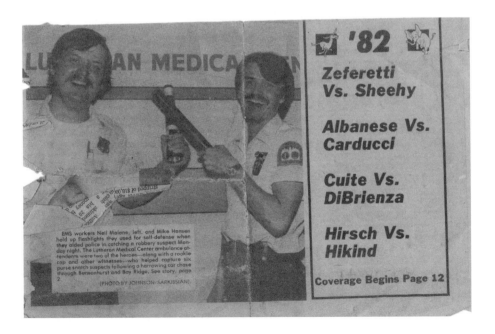

EMS workers Neil Malone, left, and Mike Hansen hold up flashlights they used for self-defense when they aided police in catching a robbery suspect Monday night. The Lutheran Medical Center ambulance attendants were two of the heroes—along with a rookie cop and other witnesses—who helped capture six purse snatch suspects following a harrowing car chase through Bensonhurst and Bay Ridge. See story, page 7.

(PHOTO BY JOHNSON-SARKISSIAN)

'82

Zeferetti Vs. Sheehy

Albanese Vs. Carducci

Cuite Vs. DiBrienza

Hirsch Vs. Hikind

Coverage Begins Page 12

Nab 6 Robbery Suspects After Car Chase

By JOHN MESAGNO

A rookie cop, two EMS ambulance workers and a private cab driver pursued and helped capture six purse snatch suspects who robbed a woman Saturday night in Bensonhurst, and began a wild car chase through local streets that ended when the suspects were apprehended in Bay Ridge, police said.

The incident began around 10:30 p.m. when the woman was approached by the suspects in a late-model Buick on Kings Highway and West Fourth St., where she surrendered her purse to them at gunpoint, according to police.

The first person who came to the woman's aid, Victor Cedero, a driver for the nearby J and J Car Service, was in the vicinity when he observed the suspects as they were fleeing in their auto, and began to chase after them, police said.

A high-speed car chase ensued with Cedero and another witness in pursuit of the suspects' car for more than 40 blocks. The suspects reportedly ran traffic signals and went the wrong way on a one-way street as the chase proceeded in Bensonhurst along Cropsey Ave. to Bath and 14th Aves. and then into Bay Ridge on 86th St.

The others picked up the chase at Fifth Ave. and 86th St., where rookie Police Officer Samuel Whitfield, assigned to the borough Task Force out of the 72nd Precinct, and two EMS ambulance workers from Lutheran Medical Center, Neil Malone and Mike Hansen, joined to apprehend one of the suspects.

Whitfield was in the area on foot patrol, issuing a summons for a traffic violation, when he spotted the suspects' car being chased by Cedero, who was yelling, "Get them, get them," police said.

At that point, Malone and Hansen turned around their ambulance, making a U-turn to pick up Whitfield as the officer followed in the ambulance with the EMS crew.

The chase was short-lived from that point, however, as the suspects were involved in a minor accident at Fourth Ave. and one of them darted from the vehicle into a nearby pizzeria.

Malone and Hansen—with their flashlights drawn as weapons—accompanied by Whitfield, followed the suspect into the pizzeria, where the officer placed him under arrest. He was identified as Donald Scott, 19, of Sterling Pl., Brooklyn.

Police Officer Samuel Whitfield prepares to take suspect Donald Scott into custody after he fled from

There was no one injured in the accident, police said.

The other five fled on foot when their car became stuck in traffic and were later apprehended on Second Ave., and 62nd St. with assistance from police of the 68th Precinct.

They were identified as Xavier Byars, 18, of Putnam Ave., Joseph Allen, 21, of Utica Ave., Russell Williams, 17, of Utica Ave., Gene Tannis, 17, of Park Pl., and Ronald ___, 18, of Franklin Ave., all Brooklyn.

Each of the suspects was charged with second-degree robbery and possession of a dangerous weapon, according to police.

Police said neither the purse nor the gun were recovered.

pursuing witnesses to a Bay Ridge pizzeria.
(PHOTOS BY JOHNSON/SARKISSIAN)

School District To Keep

One night while working his shift on the ambulance, Neil Malone heard a broadcast over the dispatch of a rape in progress. Hearing the location of the incident, Neil realized he was nearby. He found the location and chased the perp on foot. After managing to club the perp on the collar bone with his flashlight, a chase ensued. Sprinting several blocks and hopping a fence, Neil was finally able to corner the suspect for the police. The suspect was armed with a gun...Neil was not – he had just his flashlight. These incidents and others earned Neil the nickname, "Captain Eveready." At this writing such incidents still arise for Neil though he is no longer an EMS worker. He is still a fire fighter. I, for one, am extremely honored to know him!

EMS HERO FOILS RAPE, HELPS NAB SUSPECT

By JAMES NORMAN

AN Emergency Medical Service ambulance corpsman was credited yesterday with foiling a rape in a Brooklyn schoolyard, then tracking down the alleged rapist and helping cops to nail him.

Neil Mallone was in his ambulance in the East New York section of Brooklyn at 12:45 a.m. when he and driver Leroy Hall heard a call over their police radio about a woman needing help.

The two EMS men followed police to the scene, a schoolyard on Warwick Avenue.

While they waited for officers to check one side of the building, Mallone said, he took his flashlight and searched around the other side.

"As I started to get out of the ambulance, I heard a woman screaming for help," he said.

"I shined my flashlight at the base of the building, and saw a very frightened woman with a man on top of her," Mallone added.

The corpsman said he ordered the man to stop, "but he started to pull up his pants and came at me with something in his hand.

"I stepped aside to let him pass, and as he went through the gate to the yard, I hit him in the chest with my flashlight. It knocked the wind out of him."

Mallone then chased the attacker for several blocks, keeping in touch with police with a portable radio he had borrowed earlier from the 75th Precinct station house.

The suspect, who was cornered by Officer Michael Verdi in the vacant building, later was identified as Rudolph Chirse, 18, of 436 Ashford St.

He was charged with rape and sodomy.

EMS corpsman Neil Mallone with the flashlight he used to belt a rape suspect.

He helps nab rape suspect

By MIKE SANTANGELO

An Emergency Medical Service corpsman helped police capture a suspected gun-wielding rapist yesterday morning after slugging the armed man with a flashlight, police said.

Corpsman Ned Malone heard a report of "a woman in distress" over the police radio he carries in his EMS ambulance as he and driver Leroy Hall drove along Warwick St., near Belmont Ave., shortly before 2 a.m., police said.

Realizing he was near the scene, Malone asked the driver to stop at a schoolyard where calls to the police reported a woman screaming for help.

MALONE GOT OUT OF the ambulance as Sgt. Raymond O'Donald of the Sutter Ave. station arrived in response to the call.

While O'Donald and another officer went around to the front of the school, Malone heard cries for help and called O'Donald on his walkie-talkie as he went into the yard.

He found a woman being assaulted in a doorway and as her assailant tried to run, Malone slugged him with a heavy flashlight, knocking the wind out of the suspect. He was later identified by police as Rudolf Chrise, 18.

As O'Donald ran around to the yard, the suspect got up and ran with Malone and O'Donald in hot pursuit.

After a five-block chase, the two were joined by Police Officer Michael Verdi who followed the suspect over a fence and captured him in the basement of an unoccupied building on Ashford St.

Verdi heard the radio calls on the chase as he was filling out paperwork on an earlier arrest in the Sutter Ave. station.

"I heard the call and sprinted five blocks to where they were chasing the guy," said Verdi.

"I hopped over a fence after the guy and cornered him in the basement and made the arrest after a struggle," said Verdi who suffered a broken hand in the scuffle.

"THE AMBULANCE GUY did a great job," added Verdi who had nothing but praise for Malone.

"I know it's not my job," said Malone who was afraid that he might be in line for a reprimand for leaving his ambulance.

"If I do get a reprimand I won't mind," the corpsman said, "because I feel good about what I did. It was morally right."

Lt. George McDonald of EMS put Malone's fears to rest very quickly. Instead of getting chewed out, Malone has been recommended for the service's Medal of Excellence.

The rape victim was questioned at the stationhouse and treated and released from Kings County Hospital.

Police said the victim told them she had been accosted by the suspect as she was walking home. She said he showed her a gun and demanded money and when she said she had none, he assaulted her.

Chrise was charged with rape, attempted robbery and possession of a weapon.

This is Neil Malone's graduation from the Randall's Island Fire Academy. He is in the forefront of this picture on the right – high above the ground.

POLICE DEPARTMENT, CITY OF NEW YORK

Certificate of Commendation

awarded to

Neil Malone ~

in recognition of valuable assistance rendered to the members of the Police Department and to the City of New York

POLICE COMMISSIONER

DATE
December 10, 1974

Above is a Certificate of Commendation. Neil Malone received this special honor at the young age of 16! He witnessed a homicide. He alerted the police right away. The perps were still in the area and he was able to point them out to the police. His testimony solidified the guilty verdict. His first of many heroic feats – his life path set in motion.

POLICE HONOR EMS HEROS

Photo by David Burns

After the ceremony the six EMS honored posed with the Police Commissioner. From the left they are, Corpsman Neil P. Malone, Paramedic Vincent Merola, Commissioner Robert J. McGuire, Paramedic David Lerich, Corpsmen Michael D. Greenberg and Patricia M. Borrero and Paramedic Edward Orski.

At a ceremony held at One Police Plaza on November 17th, Mayor Edward I. Koch and Police Commissioner Robert J. McGuire honored six EMS Corpsmen and Paramedics for performing distinguished acts of public service that provided assistance to the police department.

Each of the six received the department's civilian commendation award.

Corpsman Neil P. Malone, who works out of the Liberty Outpost in Brooklyn, was honored for stopping a rape in progress and then assisting the police in apprehending the perpetrator.

Paramedics David Lerich and Vincent Merola, working out of Coney Island Hospital at the time, rescued two police officers who had been trapped in their vehicle after an auto accident.

Paramedic Edward Orski was honored for assisting the police in the arrest of three muggers in Central Park. Orski, then a Corpsman, was working out of Metropolitan Hospital.

Corpsmen Patricia M. Borrero and Michael D. Greenberg, then working out of Mary Immaculate Hospital, helped the police apprehend a man with a sawed-off shotgun.

Neil Malone – Medal Day Book 1988.

Subway miracle man

AUG, 7th

A man plunged off a Brooklyn subway platform yesterday — and miraculously escaped serious injury as three cars rolled over him, authorities said.

But a firefighter who was pulling the man out from under the train suffered an electric shock during the rescue.

Both men were taken to Lutheran Medical Center after the 7:35 p.m. incident at the Union Street station on Fourth Avenue.

The firefighter, Neil Malone, was admitted for observation. The unidentified man who fell onto the tracks was being evaluated but did not appear to suffer any serious injuries.

"He's an extremely lucky man," said hospital spokesman Myles Davis.

Transit Authority spokesman James Anyansi said the power had been turned off during the rescue, and authorities were investigating whether the firefighter brushed against a power box that still had live residual electricity.

Anyansi said it was not clear if the straphanger fell or jumped.

Cathy Burke

This is the article telling of Neil's electric shock he suffered on August 6, 2001. He took 600 volts through his right arm! He spent several days in the hospital. This is one of many miracles in his life. He was on medical leave for one full year but managed to work his way back in to full duty. He suffered equilibrium problems at first and non-stop migraine headaches. His short term memory suffered. Though he has recovered amazingly well, after five years he still feels pain in his right arm and seems to have extra static electricity.

Neil Malone is pictured here in a quiet moment of reflection when he attended the December 8, 2001 Memorial Ceremony at Pelco. When he mentioned this picture to me he said his friends told him he looked like an altar boy. Incidentally, he was an altar boy for several years.

Above is a collage of memories regarding fallen fire fighter Michael Bocchino. Neil sent this to me when he sent shirts for myself and Mr. McDonald. This is the time Neil also sent the card to Mr. McDonald telling him a bit of his story. Michael Bocchino was Neil's best friend, killed on 9/11. They worked out of the same firehouse. From the pictures, you see just what a special man Michael was and the close bond between him and Neil.

Me with the four musketeers at Pelco's Memorial Dedication entitled "From Sea to Shining Sea" at their location in Orangeburg, NY. From left to right are: Roman Ducalo, Eileen Gregan, myself, Neil Malone and Harry Gillen. These four are the best of friends, traveling everywhere together. Buddy and Harry are retired. Eileen is an aide to the 33rd Battalion. She drives the Chief. Neil works in the same firehouse where Buddy used to work. As a young boy, Neil would hang out at that firehouse which happens to be right around the block from where he grew up, and Buddy would kick him out! Today they are very good friends.

June 28, 2006, was a sweltering hot day in Brooklyn. Neil Malone's company was called out to a collapsed construction site. When Engine 239 arrived, the site was still unstable, a second collapse imminent. Neil saw a hand sticking out of the rubble and with quick thinking and reflexes dove in. One worker was buried up to his head. Another was buried up to his neck. The two buried men happened to be brothers – immigrants from Mexico. Neil dug dirt with his hands away from the head and face of the more seriously buried one. He held his hand to give comfort and to know that the guy was still alive. Both men were saved. The whole ordeal lasted about 2½ hours. It took a large number of rescue workers – several companies were called to the scene. The brothers were not seriously injured. Neil was taken to the hospital and kept overnight for heat exhaustion and dehydration. As of this writing, Neil has been written up for a "Class 2" Medal of Honor for his heroics. He keeps on saving lives.

 **FIRE DEPARTMENT**

To: Michael, F. Marrone   Title: 11th. Division Commander

From: Edward Watt

Date: 03/13/2007

Subject: Meritorious Acts

Please Resubmit F.F. Neil Malone, Report Of Meritorious Act , To The Board Of Merit. Reason Being, All Of His Original Paper Work Was Lost.

Respectfully Submitted,

Captain *Edward Watt* Gr #4 , E-239

BP-166 (12/00)

REPORT OF MERITORIOUS ACT   <u>July 3, 2006</u>
                                                                    Date

1.   BOX   <u>1326</u>   BOROUGH <u>Brooklyn</u>   DATE   <u>6/27/2006</u>   TIME   <u>1036</u>
        (highest alarm)

2.   PERFORMED BY: <u>FF-1</u>   <u>Neil Malone</u>   <u>E-239</u>
                            Rank or Grade   Name   Unit Assigned   Detailed

3.   DID ANY OTHER MEMBER PARTICIPATE IN THIS ACT? <u>Yes</u>

     (If Yes) _____ <u>Several Members Of Rescue 2</u> _____
                        Rank   Name   Unit

     Is Meritorious Act Report being forwarded for participating member? <u>No</u>

     If not, how did member participate? <u>Assisted in final removal of victim</u>

3a. ARE ANY UNIT CITATIONS BEING RECOMMENDED IN CONNECTION WITH THIS FIRE?____ <u>Yes</u>
     (If Yes - List Units) <u>E-279, L-131, Rescue 2</u>

4   LOCATION OF MERITORIOUS ACT
     a) If in building: Address _____ _____
         Height _____ Area _____ Construction _____
         Occupancy _____ Number of apartments in building _____
         Floor where act took place _____ Room _____

     b) If not in building: Give complete descriptive information so that physical setting can be recreated
         Excavation trench at the site of 145 11 Street between 2 Ave and 3 Ave

5.   PERSON(S) AIDED:

NAME	Manuel Vergara	Herbierto Vergara
ADDRESS	Unknown	Unkown
AGE - SEX	33 / Male	27 / Male
RESCUE BREATHING	No	No
EXTERNAL CARDIAC MASSAGE	No	No
RESUSCITATOR APPLIED	Oyxgen Applied	Oxygen Applied
HOSPITALIZED	Yes	Yes
NAME OF HOSPITAL	Lutheran Medical Cent	Lutheran Medical Cent
DIAGNOSIS	Unknown	Unknown
LENGTH OF HOSPITALIZATION	Unknown	Unknown

6.   MEMBER PERFORMING ACT: Did he receive any emergency treatment?   <u>Yes</u>
     Specify <u>Transported to hospital/ addmitted overnight</u>
     Was medical leave granted?   <u>Yes</u>   Diagnosis <u>Unkown</u>

7.   WHAT SPECIFIC JOB WAS MEMBER PERFORMING AT TIME OF RESCUE? <u>Digging victim out of collapsed</u>
     <u>excavation</u>
     WAS MEMBER ALONE? <u>No</u> (If not, indicate number of fire department personnel in immediate area, and describe
     their position in #11.
     WAS A MASK WORN BY MEMBER DURING RESCUE? _____ <u>No</u>
     WAS CHARGED HOSELINE IN POSITION TO PROTECT MEMBER MAKING RESCUE? <u>Yes</u>
     HOW WAS VICTIM REMOVED FROM PREMISE?   Carried ☒   Dragged ☐   Assisted ☐
     WAS A LADDER USED IN THIS RESCUE? <u>No</u> If yes, indicate type, size and placement

-2-
REPORT OF MERITORIOUS ACT

Neil Malone
Name of Member
5/27/2006
Date of Act

8.   NAME(S) OF TWO MEMBERS WHO ACUALLY WITNESSED ACT(IF AVAILABLE)
        RANK   NAME   UNIT

            Captain   Paul Conlon   E-239/E-207
            Lt.   Lt. Dan Murphy   R-2

9.   NAME(S) OF TWO CIVILIANS WHO ACUALLY WITNESSED ACT(IF AVAILABLE)
                    NAME   ADDRESS

            John Connolly

10.   WAS VICTIM REMOVED FROM: Immediate fire area ☐   Directly above fire ☐

      Other area (specify in detail):
      Victim was dug out of earth, bricks and concrete that had collapsed on him while working in excavation
      trench of construction site.

11.   DESCRIPTION OF ACT:

      E-239 responded to an EMS run for "Major Trauma". Upon arrival we found that an excavation trench
being dug parallel to the street at the above location had collapsed. The trench was approximately 70' long
by 15' wide by 12' deep. We saw one victim buried up to his face in the bottom of the trench. Captain
Conlon asked if their were additional victims. John Connolly, the construction supervisor, replied that there
was one additional victim and pointed to a patch of dirt approximately 20' from the visible victim.
      FF Neil Malone, without regard for for his own safety, immediately entered the trench. He quickly
determined that the visible victim, Herbierto Vergara, was breathing and then he began digging for the
completely buried victim in the area indicated by Connolly. E-239 placed a portable ladder into the trench,
stretched a precautionary 1 3/4" hoseline and passed shovels and the Oxygen bottle into the hole. FF
Malone found the completely submerged victim's hand and yelled out that he had a firm grip; he was still
alive. FF Malone dug frantically while kneeling in the bottom of the unshored and recently collapsed
excavation trench, putting himself at great personal risk, in an effort to reach the victims mouth and nose
to allow him to continue to breath. He finally reported that he had exposed the victims mouth but the victim
refused the Oxygen mask. FF Malone stated that the victims grip was getting less firm and he continued to
clear the earth around his head and face.
      As the additional units arrived at the scene and as the operation expanded and the excavation was
expertly shored up by Rescue 2 and the other SOC/ SOC support units, FF Malone continued to dig. When
pressed to rotate out of the hole for relief, he requested to stay. He said he promised the trapped worker
that he would not leave him until he was rescued. He continued to dig and operate with Lt. Murphy from R-
2, and after approximately 1 1/2 hours of non-stop effort, Manuel Vergara was freed from the location where
he was buried. The victim was secured to a stokes stretcher and carried to a waiting ambulance. FF Malone
attempted to climb from the hole but collasped and was carried to another ambulance by FD and EMS
personnel. He was admitted to the Cardiac Care Unit of Lutheran Hospital where he spent the night.
      Many dedicated, talented and well-trained members of Engines, Ladders and Rescue companies worked
under difficult circumstances to successfully rescue both victims at this incident. I have no doubt that
without the quick action of FF Malone in the first few critical minutes of this operation, that the chances of

-3-
REPORT OF MERITORIOUS ACT

Neil Malone
Name of Member
6/27/2006
Date of Act

12. DIAGRAM OF APARTMENT OR AREA FROM WHICH VICTIM WAS REMOVED

Indicate location of victim by **X**
Indicate path of entrance to apartment (or area) by **solid line**.
Indicate path of exit (if different than entrance) by **broken line**.
Indicate point of origin of fire (if known) by − with floor # inside.
Indicate area of fire by ////////
indicate location of hoseline by →   →   →
Diagram shall include all means of access to area (doors, fire escapes).

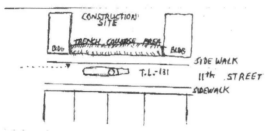

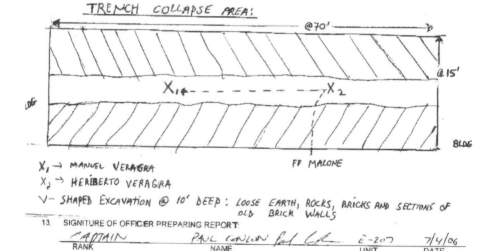

X_1 → MANUEL VERAGRA
X_2 → HERIBERTO VERAGIRA

V- SHAPED EXCAVATION @ 10' DEEP : LOOSE EARTH, ROCKS, BRICKS AND SECTIONS OF OLD BRICK WALLS

13. SIGNITURE OF OFFICER PREPARING REPORT:

CAPTAIN	PAUL CONLON	E-207	7/4/06
RANK	NAME	UNIT	DATE

-4-
REPORT OF MERITORIOUS ACT

Neil Malone
Name of Member
6/27/2006
Date of Act

14. BATTALION CHIEF ENDORSEMENT.   I was ___✓___ at scene, observed act
_____ at scene, did not observe act but investigated at scene
_____ not at scene. Investigated

Conclusion regarding facts of the Meritorious Act.

I concur with the facts as stated. It is my belief that FF Malone's quick action & disregard for his own safety was instrumental in the success of this operation.

B.C.   John Martarana   13.32   7/7/06
RANK   NAME   UNIT   DATE

14. DEPUTY CHIEF ENDORSEMENT.   I was ___X___ at scene, observed act
_____ at scene, did not observe act but investigated at scene
_____ not at scene. Investigated

Conclusion regarding facts of the Meritorious Act.

FF Malone, upon seeing the trapped and distressed victim jumped into a very unstable and still collapsing trench. He operated without regard for his own safety to attend to the visible victim. He then proceeded under a large and unstable slab of concrete and beside to dig and expose the second victim who was completely buried and close to suffocation. Had FF Malone not placed himself at great personal risk this second victim certainly would have succumbed.

RECOMMENDATION: CLASS I _____   CLASS II __X__   CLASS III _____
SERVICE RATING A _____   B _____   FILE _____

D.C.   D-11   7/18/06
RANK   NAME   UNIT   DATE

Malone

FIRE DEPARTMENT
750 Main Street Roosevelt Island, NY 10004
TEL. 212 570-9440   FAX 212 750-2787

SPECIAL OPERATIONS COMMAND

TO: Officers and Members
            Rescue 2
            Rescue 5
            Squad 1
            Engine 239
            Ladder 132
            EMS Units
            CON-ED Crew

FROM: William A. Siegel   Deputy Chief

DATE: July 1, 2006

SUBJECT: Trench Job

"Tuesday June 27th was a lucky day for the two construction workers that were buried in the trench at 45 11th Street Brooklyn."

I want to compliment the members involved in this successful removal operation for their outstanding efforts at a tough job. It just seemed that everything went right. That everyone operated professionally and that these two people were the benefactors of some of the best training, equipment and leadership the City of New York has to offer.

I compliment the Company Officers for their training efforts and the style of leadership displayed. We all compliment the Firefighters for their knowledge of the equipment and procedures used at this type of incident. Their ability to stay focused during this type of operation is outstanding. We also must take note of the excellent job done by the EMS workers and the rapid response and support by the CON ED crew.

Congratulations to everyone for a job well done.

Chief of Rescue Operations

William A. Siegel   7/1/06

William A. Siegel   Date

APPENDIX II

TRIBUTES

A FIREMAN'S PRAYER

When I am called to duty, God
Wherever Flames may rage
Give me the strength to save some life
Whatever Be its age
Help me embrace a little child
Before it is too late
Or save an older person from
The horror of that fate
Enable me to be alert and
Hear the weakest shout
And quickly and efficiently
To put the fire out
I want to fill my calling and
To give the best in me
To guard my every neighbor
And protect their property
And if according to your will
I have to lose my life
Please bless with your protecting hand
My children and my wife

THANK YOU FOR YOUR SUPPORT.

©2001 The Record (Bergen County, NJ)
Photo by Thomas E. Franklin,
Staff Photographer

Photo taken September 11, 2001 at the World
Trade Center and published in The Record on
September 12, 2001

August 6, 2004

Dear Sue,

RE: Lt Joseph Agnello
     FDNY LADDER 118

Thank You for contacting my contacting my mother regarding the book of 911 Heros. We will cherish and keep it close to our hearts.

My brother was appointed to FDNY on July 25, 1993. He received one commendation for meritorious service. Joe always was a special person. When he was an 18 year old kid, he survived being attacked with a knife. Joe help a friend in trouble. The

injuries he suffered were so
sever that last rights were
administered.

Joe was so proud to be a
New York City fireman. He passed
the lieutenant to twice, and on
September 11, 2001 the department
promoted him to Lieutenant. A
goal he proudly strove for.

God Bless
Rosaria Agrello Nastingane

FDNY Lt. Joseph Agnello

Stephen Patrick Driscoll

Born on the 4th day of July, 1963
Born into everlasting life on the 11th day of September, 2001
Found & brought home on the 8th day of November, 2001
Laid to rest on the 14th day of November, 2001
World Trade Center

This thank you comes from our hearts. Thank you for your prayers and kind words. We were given these words of comfort and in turn would like to pass them onto you, our family and friends:

Feel no guilt in laughter
They know how much you care
Feel no sorrow in a smile
That they're not here to share
You cannot grieve forever
They would not want you to
They'd hope that you would carry on
The way you always do
So talk about the good times
And the ways you showed you cared
The days you spent together
All the happiness you shared
Let memories surround you
A word someone may say
Will suddenly recapture
A time, an hour, a day
That brings them back as clearly
As though they were still here
And fills you with the feelings
That they are always near
For if you keep those moments
You will never be apart
And they will live forever
Locked safe within you heart.

Love Letitia & Patrick Driscoll
36 Lake Shore Drive East
Lake Carmel, NY 10512

TA 900236 *Time*

OVERTIME REPORT *Log# 15608*
PD 138-064 (Rev. 7-87)-13   (SUBMIT THIS REPORT IMMEDIATELY)

RANK	SOCIAL SECURITY NO.	COMMAND
Po	*111-58-3592*	*884*

SHIELD	SURNAME	FIRST	M.I.
17482	*Drisone*	*Charles*	

SQD./CHT.	TOUR NUMBER
3/P8	*3*

TIME ACTUALLY WORKED	DATE FROM	DATE TO	HRS.	MIN.
	9/0 01	*9/0 01*		
	TIME *0700*	TIME *1705*	*10*	*05*

TIME SCHEDULED TO WORK	DATE FROM	DATE TO	HRS.	MIN.
	9/0 01	*9/0 01*		
	TIME *0700*	TIME *1535*	*8*	*35*

COMPENSATION OPTION (Check One)	OVERTIME PER-FORMED	HRS.	MIN.
☑TIME ☐CASH		*1*	*30*

TRAVEL TIME (IF APPLICABLE)

CMD./LOCATION WHERE DUTY PERFORMED *884 6*

INCIDENT TIME (Actual time of occurrence) *1500*

REASON FOR LOST TIME: (Identify incident specifically)
LTPK IDD Job and Sty from 6 PM and 688

I hereby certify that this report is accurate:

Date	Rank/Signature of Requesting Member
9/0 01	*B SPD*

SUPERVISORY OFFICER'S CERTIFICATION
O/T EARNED: ☐ OUTSIDE DETAIL   ☐ PERMANENT COMMAND

DETAIL SUPERVISOR: If member returns to command, do not sign form. Record time member directed to command. | DETAIL SUPERVISOR: If member is released from outside detail, sign and record time dismissed.
        Hrs.   Hrs.

CHECK ONE: ☐ DETAIL COMMAND LOG ☐ PCT COMMAND LOG	TIME OF ENTRY *1705*	DATE *9/0 01*	PAGE NO. *320*

Date	Supervisor's Name Printed	Command
9/0 01	*Sgt Horn*	*E-4*

Rank/Signature of Supervisor *Sgt Horn*

INSTRUCTIONS: Submit pink copy to desk officer or supervisor at time of FINAL dismissal. Form must be certified by a supervisor and returned to member for submission to permanent command.

Home | Memorial Pages | Events | Search | Newsletter | Contact Info

Home Page
Memorial Pages
Sponsor A Hero
Contribute
Your Thoughts
About 9-11-01
Of Interest
Events
Search Site
Contact Info
Links

FDNY'S TRAUMA ON RISE

By DAN KADISON

PAIN:
Our Bravest are still reeling from 9/11.
AP

February 18, 2003 --
One firefighter has become a "horror" who "lives on anti-depressants." Another wishes he could just retire. And another described himself as "on a roller coaster" of fear and alcohol abuse.

These are just three of the thousands of city firefighters who, medical experts say, are increasingly angry, anxious and frightened some 17 months after the World Trade Center was destroyed.

The pain can manifest itself in many ways - from feeling unsocial at a party to a full-blown case of post-traumatic stress disorder. Experts describe the firefighters' emotions as similar to soldiers in front-line combat.

What they're going through is "very typical after this kind of trauma," said Dr. James Gordon, director of the Washington-based Center for Mind-Body Medicine.

"The amount of loss was enormous," Gordon said, referring to the 343 city firefighters who died on Sept. 11, 2001.

Firefighters don't normally talk about their torment. Many fear that showing what is seen as weakness will lose them the trust of their colleagues.

But with the pain still so great, a few are willing to speak out - anonymously.

One firefighter said he has undergone therapy and medication, but it hasn't helped.

"I'm sometimes scared," he said. "I'm on a roller coaster that won't stop."

He also said he's concerned about his co-workers' "massive consumption of alcohol."

Another just wants out of his job.

"I wish I can fall off the Fire Department map," he said, choking back tears. "I need to be with my family."

The wife of another firefighter doesn't know how much longer her marriage can last. "He's a wreck. He's a horror to live with," she said.

On 9/11, her husband arrived at the World Trade Center as the first tower fell. For days, the firefighter - now on medical leave - carried out his dead comrades and parts of their bodies.

First came the nightmares. Then the depression and anger.

"He lives on anti-depressants and sleeping pills," she said.

Last month, Malachy Corrigan, director of the FDNY Counseling Services Unit, listed the primary diagnoses of the 3,800 firefighters, officers and EMS responders his office saw between Sept. 11, 2001, and Dec. 31, 2002.

The top five primary diagnoses were anxiety (roughly 1,400 cases); marital and couple problems (800); alcohol problems (400); depression (320); and post-traumatic stress disorder (230).

"We know it's there, but we don't discuss it," said Lt. Kevin Guy, who retired in November because of asthma. "How could anybody not be affected by [9/11]?"

Return to Of Interest Page

Dear Commanding Officer-

I'm writing to say thank you, and to let you know that in central California — at a company called Pelco — there are thousands of people thinking of you daily, and sending their support.

I have enclosed a few copies of our recent company newsletter, the Pelco Press. This special issue has been distributed to many thousands of our friends, colleagues and customers in the security industry — and we are all united in our pride and support for your tireless efforts.

Please feel free to order additional copies if you like, at no charge of course, but the purpose of this letter is to simply let you know that you are in our thoughts and prayers.

Sincerely,

Howard Carder,
Pelco Marketing Manager

This is the letter that accompanied our Special Edition Pelco Press (Oct 1, 2001) that was sent to all the firehouses and precincts in New York.

February 2002

Dear Sue:

I've just received your letter, what an amazing story. Talking with you over the phone I would've never realized the ordeal that you had undergone, I must say it was very uplifting.

There is no doubt in any ones mind that what happened here on the 11th was a tragedy beyond words. As a result we the FDNY became known as heroes, I for one am not deserving of such honor, the honor goes to the ones that we lost, all 343, they are the true heroes. Thank you anyway.

We could never thank the entire staff at Pelco and the city of Fresno enough for what they did for the FDNY back in December. You've helped with the healing process. Thank you very much for the letter and the prayers.

> Your friend
> Firefighter Stan Aviles
> Engine 43
> FDNY

Ps enclosed you will find a piece of wtc glass I came across while working at the site

Dear Sue,

First I must apologize for not getting back to you sooner. The material you sent me was recieved with great enthusiasm, I could not pass it around fast enough. All of the people who got a copy of it were overwhelemed by the wondefull thing the people of California did for our fallen fire, police and EMS. The most moving one is the cover with the firemen raising the flag on one of the towers, if you have more please send them.

Please accept the two CDs as our thanks for all your work. One is a grouping of photos taken by FDNY, NYPD, EMS, news agencies, and civilians. There is a large amount of material on this CD so take your time and explore all the different folders. Keep in mind some of the photos are very graphic.

The other CD are photos that the Cooperstown Fire Dept. and EMS took while we at the WTC on Sept . 18-19-20.

Thank you again for all you have done. Please stay in contact with us , we would like to here more about your company and all the wonderful things you do.

From the crew of CFD A-195, with all our love and thanks,

Wolfgang

MY BRAIN AND THE LACK THEREOF

Sue Okenyi

Ann Rewalt

1118 St. Agnes Drive

Green Bay, Wisconsin, 54304

1880 Words

JUST A SLIGHT IMPERFECTION --- BUT!

The miracle of life is followed by the wonder of growth and development in the normal child.

I doubt if anyone ever appreciated seeing a loved one live, grow, and develop more than did my husband, Ray, and I.

Six years after our boy was born,
we were blessed with a beautiful baby girl with a
perfectly round face, plump and pleasant and angelic.
But something, somehow, marred this masterpiece
of life.

When Sue was shown to me in the
delivery room she was a slightly blue but very
lively baby. I was so happy! She was finally
here for us to love, cuddle and care for. But
I couldn't hold her close, cuddle her for what
seemed like ages, though it was actually only
a little more than a week. Then I did so with
love, pain, and fear.

She was born with what seemed to be
just a little extra -- a small golf-ball-sized sac
at the center back of her head. It looked like
it could be snipped off neatly with a sterilized
scissors. Then Sue would be just like any other
infant. When that remedy occurred to me I feared
the doctor would do just that. Was there brain
involvement? If the sac were removed, what would
this do to her chances for normal mentality?

Ann Rewalt   Page 3

        I tried to vision her growing up
with her 'flesh ponytail.' Would she break it?
Toddlers fall often. How could she live with it?
This wasn't a likely solution. Was there a
solution? What was it?

        I left her at the hospital after
four days and went home with no idea if she would
ever come home to us, with no knowledge of what her
problem really was, with no answers to my many
questions. I did not find out definitely until
she was eight days old that her problem did
involve her brain. My fears were confirmed ---
I wasn't imagining things.

        Small comfort to us at this time
was the knowledge that there are certain areas
of the brain that can be spared, areas that are
not necessary for 'normal mentality.'

        When Sue was ten days old the
sac was removed, much as I thought it could be,
but only after careful tests and examinations by
a neurosurgeon and several other doctors.

Ann Rewalt   Page 4

        She came out of surgery with a
healthy appetite and seemingly good health.
Then our concern was not so much in what we did
know but in the lack of explanation from the
doctors about what to expect in the future.
No one ever assured us that she was all right
now, that we should relax and enjoy our baby,
that she would be fine.

        What was wrong? Didn't the
doctors care about our nerves? Didn't they
realize the concern and worry we felt?

        They did. They didn't want to
allow us to make plans nor expect too happy a
future for our daughter.

        Time passed and then the full
truth was revealed to us. We felt no relief
in the terrible tension we lived with. Sue
was hydrocephalic. Only time and then tests
could tell the doctors this for certain. The
truth came when she was nineteen days old.

        When active, hydrocephalus (water
head) is a building up of spinal fluid in the

Ann Rewalt   Page 5

chambers of the brain creating pressure on brain
cells, a pressure which destroys the cells and
causes retardation and eventually death.

There was a possibility of saving
her life and mentality but only a possibility.
It involved subjecting our tiny infant to a three
hour operation. An operation which would place
a small nickel sized valve in the side of her
head, a tube from that valve into her brain and
another tube from the valve through the jugular
vein and into her heart. A frightening thought,
to us, to happen to anyone, but to our baby ---
she was less than three weeks old!

We were shocked to be faced with
such an ordeal --- this couldn't be happening to
us! The expense was a concern to us too, but we
felt it was our only chance to have two children
in our family --- we had waited so long between
them and our chances of having more were very
slim.

Sue came home from the hospital
on New Year's Day, 1964, two days before she was
a month old. We were ready for her but not for
what was yet to come.

Ann Rewalt   Page 6

I was to be prepared for the fact that she might have convulsions -- I saw her in convulsions three times following her second trip to surgery and knew I would recognize them.

I had to gently pump the valve with my finger three times a day and measure her head every few days, recording the measurement. I was to watch for excessive vomiting and high pitched crying.

This baby was, from the day of her birth, a very peaceful and quiet child who seldom cried -- she was so easily pleased. We became so very close to her, she was so completely lovable.

The day that the valve wouldn't be pumped I became alarmed and took her to the doctor immediately. At that point he could not be certain yet that there was any reason to be alarmed but told me to report anything unusual to him.

Ann Rewalt   Page 7

Within a week she was spitting
up regularly and I used more diapers catching
and cleaning up the rejected milk than I did
on her bottom.

The doctor didn't need an examination when I took her in to his office to
know that the hydrocephalus was active and that
the valve was not functioning. This was obvious
by the bulging veins on her forehead and temples,
by the tilt of her eyes and by the measurement
record I showed him.

He advised us not to repeat the
surgery -- that our chances were very poor of
being successful.

By the time she was three months
old she was placed in a state hospital, with
the future supposedly short and requiring medical
attention and care, a care beyond even the love
of a mother and father.

Ray and I sat in the car outside
the hospital after leaving her and cried -- the
first we were able to since she was nineteen

Ann Rewalt   Page 8

days old. We were wound up so tightly we hadn't
relaxed for two and a half months -- it seemed
like forever.

        We dreaded the long ride home,
the beginning of adjusting to possibly never
seeing our child alive again. So we went bowling. ----Yes, bowling, five games each. And we
bowled to relax every chance we had for the next
three months. We bowled four times a week ---
sometimes together, other times completely alone.
Our bowling didn't improve much but we were able
to be reasonably cheerful and controlled during
that time. Our relatives cried, couldn't converse
with friends, even with us, about Sue without
some tear shedding.

        For the first time in our lives
Ray and I realized that people do what they have
to do, what they need to do, when they are under
tension. We didn't, couldn't worry about what
people thought of us. And we prayed. I realize
now better than ever before that prayer helps
the nerves as well as the soul.

Ann Rewalt   Page 9

        After a few trips to see her we noticed no real change in her. Each succeeding trip exploited our parental love, demanding super-efforts to resettle our nerves afterwards. My prayers were no longer for strength to hold up under the strain but rather that God speed up whatever He had in mind so that we could accept it and return to a more settled life. At that time I was willing to accept her death or her life but I wanted to be freed from this endlessly upheavaled life.

        Exactly three months after Sue entered the hospital she was released to us on an extended vacation. She was six months old.

        Sue, contrary to the fearful, and perhaps pessimistic diagnosis, was no longer regressing but rather, slowly progressing. She was, for what reason we don't know, no longer an active hydrocephalic. Her head was growing at nearly an average rate. She learned to turn from her back to her stomach -- progress -- small but definite.

Progress was slow. She was eleven months old before she could sit up alone. At a year she had only one tooth.

Then, when she was fifteen months old, her leg turned blue as she tried to support her weight of 33 pounds. Immediately came doubts of whether she would ever be able to support her weight. What was wrong? Would she ever walk?

The doctor advised removal of the valve system saying that it could be interferring with her circulation and since she no longer was using it, the logical thing was to remove it. We knew all along that this would someday be necessary anyway.

She was in surgery less than 30 minutes. The doctor told us that to his great surprise he had discovered excessive pressure as he removed the system. To us and to him this was cause for great alarm.

For three days we lived in terror-- we were back to the tension experienced in Sue's first month of life. If what the doctor suspected

Ann Rewalt   Page 11

was true, that the hydrocephalus was again active, there would be definite evidence of it in a matter of days.

So, we watched. She awakened from surgery bright and cheerful, giggling at the antics of one of her room-mates -- more active than ever. The afternoon following her surgery she tried to pull herself up in her crib -- the first time she had ever done this. She also brought herself up to a sitting position -- alone -- another first for her.

After four days in the hospital Sue came home to us again from her third hospital experience! Three times we had had to prepare ourselves for the end of her life. Three times her life had been spared.

Then we had to resume every day living and we did just that. However, we became very alarmed a few times. A few months after her third operation Sue awakened at 4 a.m. screaming and vomiting. We did what we could to comfort her and tried to believe it wasn't reactivated

Ann Rewalt   Page 12

hydrocephalus. In the morning we called a doctor
and found that she had an ear infection, which
relieved us unbelievably. The second time it
happened we weren't quite as frightened but never-
the-less an ear examination by the doctor was as
helpful to our nerves as any tranquilizer.

At twenty months she began walking
alone, cautiously as she does most things.

Yes, she did suffer setbacks; she
is behind in some things but she is progressing
and that is important.

Today, at two years of age, Sue is
a bright and pleasant little girl. She counts
2, 3, 4, 3, 7, 12, 10 and holds her own in family
conversation, truly feminine.

We parents have made progress, too.
We have learned much from this experience. We
have gained confidence in ourselves; we have
discovered our ability to face crises, keep our
heads, hold up under an extended period of strain.
We are stronger people, cautious, but not as
frightened of tomorrow. +

The State of Wisconsin

CENTRAL WISCONSIN COLONY
AND
TRAINING SCHOOL

MADISON (4)

March 4, 1964

Mr. and Mrs. Raymond Rewalt
1118 St.Agnes Drive
Green Bay, Wisconsin

                                    Re: Sue Ellen Rewalt
                                          BD 12-2-63

Dear Mr. and Mrs. Rewalt:

I am writing to make an appointment with you for Sue Ellen's
admission to Central Colony. We are expecting you to bring
her here on Monday, March 9 at 1:30 PM. I trust that this
appointment will be convenient for you.

Please bring only the outfit of clothing which she is wearing
that day. If she is currently on medication, please bring a
copy of the physician's prescription for this medication. We
would also appreciate receiving one or two of her favorite toys;
washable toys are best and something that would hang from her
crib would also be appropriate.

Unless I hear from you to the contrary, I will expect you on the
9th. Please enter the main door at the far north of the Colony
grounds and ask for me at our reception area.

                                    Sincerely,

                                    Peter W. Townsend, ACSW
                                    Social Worker

PWT:bjm

CC: T. Dettweiler
     Dr. R. Gruesen

The State of Wisconsin
CENTRAL WISCONSIN COLONY
AND
TRAINING SCHOOL
MADISON (4)

May 26, 1964

Mr. and Mrs. Raymond Rewalt
1118 St. Agnes Drive
Green Bay, Wisconsin

                              Re: Sue Ellen Rewalt
                                  CWC 5-696

Dear Mr. and Mrs. Rewalt:

We are happy to grant permission for Sue Ellen to visit with you
for an extended vacation beginning Monday, June 8, 1964. As
arranged we will expect you to arrive between noon and 2:00 PM.

If these plans need modification kindly contact me.

We share your trust that Sue will continue to make progress
and that she will continue in good health.

                              Sincerely,

                              Harvey A. Stevens
                              Superintendent

CMW:bjm

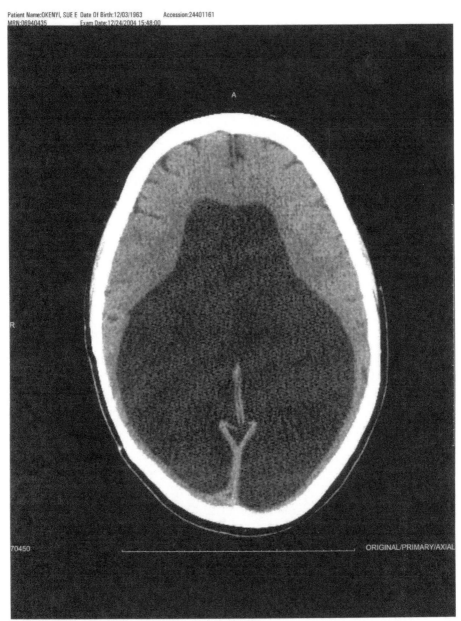

70450   ORIGINAL/PRIMARY/AXIAL

APPENDIX IV

TOM O'NEILL

This is the flag Tom recovered from the mud at Ground Zero. Tom is in the middle behind the flag. Paul Sweeney is on the left. All the guys from Paul's unit signed the flag. They were presenting the flag to Tom and Tom had it presented to Engine 167 Ladder 87.

Pictures of Paul Sweeney with his U.S. Army Special Forces Unit. He took the flag that Tom recovered from Ground Zero to Afghanistan and Iraq.

Tom on the job. He worked as a Communications Engineer.

Flag presentation to Tom O'Neill at Engine 167 in Staten Island.

From left: Patty Duffy, Neadly Foster, Fran O'Neill, myself. Eric Duffy is seated.

APPENDIX V

LETTERS

May 27, 2003

Mrs. Sue Okenyi
Pelco World Headquarters
3500 Pelco Way
Clovis, CA   93612-5699

Dear Mrs. Okenyi:

First I must apologize for having taken literally months to write to you since I last spoke to you on the telephone. I must also thank you for all of the 9/11 memorabilia, VCR tapes, CDs and literature you have sent to me, my son P.O. Michael Gerbasi and fellow Police Officer friends, who we put in contact with you.

I must also tell you how absolutely moved I was after reading the brief history of your struggles since birth. That is a real story of strength, heroism and faith.

I am enclosing some items for what I am sure has become a large personal collection of 9/11 memorabilia. The photograph of my son with Harrison Ford was taken when he appeared at Paul McCartney's Concert for New York. He was asked to introduce Eric Clapton; it is No. 23 on the DVD of the event. I am also enclosing the program from the NYPD's Medal Day held on January 17, 2003, together with a picture of him holding his award. Almost all of the recipients were 9/11 related. A brief description of Michael's incident appears at the bottom of the third from last page. Michael nominated his partner P.O. Anthony Cozzi for the award, for having saved his, Michael's, life. Upon hearing that he was to receive the award P.O. Cozzi wanted to refuse it stating that he was not deserving of the award not having been injured. Michael then reminded him of the promise they had made to each other when they partnered up, that neither one would ever desert the other in time of danger.

FYI P.O. JoAnn Spreen, who appears at the top of that same page was standing next to Michael when she was injured. Michael and JoAnn have both returned to full duty and now work in the same Task Force in lower Manhattan just blocks from Ground Zero.

-2-

What made this ceremony extra special is that it was held in the Winter Garden section of the World Financial Center which is located across West Street from where the Twin Towers once stood. The Winter Garden is a multi-story atrium, containing Palm trees, in N.Y.C., which was completely destroyed when the Towers collapsed. When standing on its marble floor and looking around it is hard to believe that all of this had been destroyed, ruble removed, rebuilt and refurbished in just sixteen months.

You might also want to note, on the second to last page that Michael's Precinct, the First, received a Unit Citation for its performance on 9/11 and post 9/11.

One item of my personal past that might be of interest to you, and will explain my personal attachment to the World Trade Center, is that from its beginning, in the early '70's, until I retired in 1991, I was the N.Y.S. Senior Public Building Manager. My responsibilities covered the operations and maintenance of all N.Y.S. occupied areas which included the 23rd to 85th floors and five sub-grade levels of Tower II, Two World Trade Center.

I also wanted to mention that I received your general letter of April 29th with reference to the Ceremony on June 14th in Orangeburg, NY. I was surprised that I received it and Michael didn't; especially since he had attended the Ceremony in Clovis, CA in December '01. My wife and I will certainly try to attend and if so, I will certainly try to search you out so that we can speak face to face and I can thank you for all you and Pelco have done for these surviving Heroes.

Hope to see you on the 14th.

Cordially yours,

Peter A. Gerbasi

34 Pashen Place
Dix Hills, NY 11746

E-Mail – pagerbasi@yahoo.com

INTER-OFFICE MEMO

To: Phil Griswa
From: Joe McDevitt
Date: September 12, 2001
Subject: Update - NY

Phil:

A quick update from Orangeburg:

The meeting with Jordan, the Statue of Liberty & Ellis Island US Park Police scheduled for today was cancelled due to the tragedy yesterday. As we understand it the Statue is secured and the US Marines are now on Liberty Island providing physical security. Ellis Island has been turned into a temporary morgue.

Several of our employees who live in NYC were unable to return home yesterday due to the closing of the bridges and tunnels leading to NYC. However, they made arrangements to stay locally and at this point all but one, Frank Valez, who lives in Manhattan has gotten back home. Frank is staying with one of our other employees, Cliff Atwater, until he can make his way back into Manhattan.

Janine Kalle', Orangeburg HR, is organizing a blood drive with the local Red Cross and most if not all of our employees will be going there today to donate. However, in trying to give blood last night at several area hospitals people were turned away simply because they were unable to handle the volume of people trying to donate. Please ask all employees in California to help in this cause, as it may be easier to donate out there. Janine is also getting information on food donations, which we will send to you as soon as possible. We would very much appreciate our Fresno family's contribution with any canned goods that could be collected.

We are all feeling a bit helpless this morning, but our past experience has surely proven that no company can pitch in and help in difficult times like Pelco. So we ask all of you to do your best in assisting with blood and food if possible.

Thank you,

Joe McDevitt

INTER-OFFICE MEMO

To: Pelco Clovis
From: Joe McDevitt
Date: September 13, 2001
Subject: State of Affairs – New York

To Our Pelco Family,

The employees from Orangeburg would like to thank you all for your well wishes, thoughts and prayers following the horrific terrorist actions in New York. As you know by now all of us are unharmed and although affected by this tragedy are in very high spirits. We have been feeling somewhat helpless over the past few days in that we were unable to lend our assistance to the residents in NYC due to logistical issues with traveling into the affected area. All that changed today and we are proud to share with you what your company has done.

Under the direction of Mr. McDonald, Pelco contacted the New York City Police Department and the United States Parks Department/Department of the Interior and offered any and all assistance possible. Our excellent relationship with these agencies prompted them to immediately accept our offer for assistance. This morning the NYPD showed up on our front door and asked for assistance with the search and rescue efforts underway in lower Manhattan. The buildings surrounding what was the World Trade Center are very unsafe and in danger of falling. This puts all of the rescue teams in great danger. So, our friends at the NYPD had an idea. They wanted to temporarily mount Spectra domes to several buildings and even to bucket trucks so that they could monitor the dangerous areas without having rescue workers in direct danger. Our people jumped all over this challenge. Each and every employee here dropped what they were doing and collected the required equipment, set-up a test bench, tested all of the equipment and even solicited the assistance of one of our customers who was here attending the CM9760 Certification class. The dealer, John Palmarie of IST, had access to wireless transmission equipment, which was needed to send the video and control data allowing the NYPD to do their jobs at a safe distance. Our local Sheriff's department pitched in providing police escort to John's offices where the wireless equipment was picked-up, brought to Orangeburg and tested before being handed over to the NYPD. A great effort extended by your fellow employees and a feeling contribution has finally been realized.

As all this was going on, Jordan Heilweil of Total Recall Corporation contacted us regarding the Statue of Liberty installation. Security had to be stepped up considerably to protect against any other possible terrorist actions and again your fellow employees met the challenge. Immediately, Tom Dodrill split our staff in two. Assigning one team to the NYPD and the other to the Statue of Liberty. equipment was stripped off the shelves, tested and dispatched to both locations. NYPD can now operate more safely and Liberty Island is now being blanketed with the highest quality Pelco equipment protecting the symbol of freedom we all know and love.

If it was the intention of these cowardly terrorists to break the will of the American people I can assure you that the result is the exact opposite. Never before have I seen so much conviction to help and assist our fellow citizens. And I want to assure you all that Pelco Blue ran as deep as it ever has on this day. A special thanks to the employees who rose to the occasion under the direction of Tom Dodrill: Walter Bayer, Lou Conte, Pedro Castillo, Evghenii Croitor, Dennis Dodrill, Kevin Galuppo, Joel Gultz, Alain Innocent, Joe LaRocco, Rich Mazzola, Kevin O'Brien, Erick Rodriguez, Nick Valerio and Jerry Winters.

Thank you all again for your thoughts and prayers. We will continue to represent Pelco with pride.

INTER-OFFICE MEMO

To: Pelco Clovis
From: Joe McDevitt
Date: September 17, 2001
Subject: Update - NY

Fellow employees:

It is with great pride that I again update you on the activities of your coworkers in NY.

On Saturday September 17, 2001 at 7:00 AM, Dennis Dodrill, Tom Dodrill and Walter Bayer arrived at what is now known as "Ground Zero." They arrived under police escort to assist the NYPD with their implementation of remote monitoring equipment to more safely carry out the duties of surveying lower Manhattan. These three employees volunteered to work alongside New York's finest, right at the heart of the disaster area. In fact as I was speaking to Dennis Dodrill by telephone on Saturday, Dennis, Walter and Tom were being evacuated from the building they were working in because of structural problems. After a 2-hour delay and countless safety inspections they were allowed to return to the top of the structure to mount the Spectra's and wireless equipment so badly needed to carry out the search and ensure the safety of rescue workers at the scene. I am happy to report that they accomplished this task and have everything operational.

To further the distances the officers can operate the equipment Walter Bayer and various members of Orangeburg Engineering again solicited the assistance of Bob Evens and John Palmarie of IST, a local Pelco dealer. IST provided additional wireless equipment and Walter and his team assembled a repeater station which could be used to repeat the signals used for video and control transmission. This now allows the NYPD to be completely mobile and deal with these evacuations more safely and efficiently.

But they didn't stop there! On Sunday morning they again went to the site to help with whatever they could and again on Monday morning as I write this update they are there. Their hard work and dedication is inspirational and I am proud, as I am sure you are, to have the privilege of working with them.

INTER-OFFICE MEMO

To: Pelco Clovis
From: Joe McDevitt
Date: September 17, 2001
Subject: Update – New York

Pitching in takes all forms today. From our previous updates you know of the efforts put forth by Pelco on a technical level to assist with safety and security around New York's Ground Zero. But today was a little different. Today a truck from our local Salvation Army showed up at our loading dock. It was filled to the top with food items, clothing, dust masks, boots, gloves, shovels, pick axes, etc.... There are literally thousands of items. The Salvation Army is receiving items like this to assist with the cleanup in NYC. And they're getting so much, so fast that they can't get it to the site fast enough and the people at the site can't use it as fast as they're getting it. So, our offer for assistance was accepted. The truckload of items is now "on ice" so to speak in Pelco's Orangeburg New York warehouse where it can be stored until the Salvation Army can work through the logistics of getting it to the people who need it.

The entire Orangeburg staff pitched in and unloaded this truck in a bucket brigade fashion (see attached pictures). Each item was palletized and organized with similar items so that they can be quickly picked, as they are needed. The truck actually originated from a community in Harrisburg Pennsylvania. The group that collected the items sent a picture (attached) signed by all saying how happy they were to be able to help. Our thanks go out to these good neighbors and our assurance that they will help many people in this time of need.

ADDITIONAL MATERIAL

St. Patrick's Day in New York

By Kent Burkhart, Clovis Firefighters, Local 1695

584 Clovis/Fresno area firefighters, police and family members flew to New York as a show of support for our New York brothers to march with them in the honorable St. Patrick's Day Parade on Saturday, March 16, 2002.

Two dates I will always remember are St. Patrick's Day and The California Memorial Dedication in Clovis on December 8. In December, Pelco, a security camera manufacturing company in Clovis, flew 1150 New York firefighters, police and Port Authority police to Clovis, all expenses paid for this beautiful 2 1/2-hour dedication ceremony. New York firefighters then invited Pelco President and CEO David McDonald to be the Honorary Grand Marshal in The Parade.

Instead of staying in hotels like everyone else, Henry Hernandez and I opted to accept the invitation of FDNY friends and stay in their homes. We stayed with F/F Rob Santandrea in Astoria for two nights, then with Lt. Dan Walsh in Staten Island for three nights. We got to know each other better, strengthening our relationships. These friendships will continue to grow as they plan to visit us in the near future.

Most Clovis/Fresno area firefighters and police arrived March 13 to meet with friends from FDNY, NYPD and PAPD made earlier in December at the California Memorial Dedication for a very large reception at Pier 90 in Manhattan which lasted until midnight. Thursday sightseeing included the WTC site, Empire State Building, and Fresh Kills landfill. That evening, David McDonald's family, Henry and I had a great dinner with Engine 45 and Ladder 58 in the Bronx and then rode along with them on calls. Mr. McDonald had the opportunity to drive Ladder Tower 58, then Ladder 27 code 3 through the Bronx, then perfectly backing Ladder Tower 58 into the station! Friday we went to several different firehouses then to have lunch with my wife's Uncle Sandy, whom I had never met

before. In his apartment in Battery Park City he showed us the window where he watched the towers fall and gave us his entire story. After we joined the group to an inspiring and memorable afternoon and evening to the Statue of Liberty, Ellis Island and dinner cruise on the Hudson River. A Fireboat filled the Manhattan skyline with several huge sprays in a salute to their California friends. The twin "light towers", visible from anywhere we were on the Hudson, were absolutely breathtaking. The Statue of Liberty close up at night is awesome.

The parade on Saturday was the largest parade I've ever seen. 200,000 marching in the parade and 2 million attending were reported. You wouldn't believe the enormous support from the public with signs, enthusiasm and cheers for their heroes. I had mixed emotions about marching with the FDNY. I felt proud and honored to march shoulder to shoulder with the "Pillars of America", yet not worthy to be with them when the enthusiastic public waved, cheered and saluted them because of who they are and what they have been through. We marched 44 blocks down 5th Avenue. The Moment of Silence I will never forget...one could hear a pin drop as everyone turned and faced south toward the towers site at 12:30. It was an incredible memory.

Most went home Sunday. But we had the honor to march in the Staten Island Parade on Sunday, an invitation from Lt. Dan Walsh we could not pass up.

We met many new friends we will see again. We consoled many who told us their story and their loss. Some even asked us to place pictures of their heroes on The Memorial, which we will and send them photographs of the formal event. We all had the experience of a lifetime, which will never be forgotten.

At left firefighters march in front of St. Patrick's Cathedral; above right fireboats in New York harbor at right the author in front of the Statue of Liberty.

Memorial CD is an inspirational fundraiser

On December 8, 2001, over one thousand New York firefighters, law enforcement officers, rescue workers and family members of fallen offic ers arrived in Central California. They came at the invitation of valley businessman David McDonald, Pres./CEO Peloo, who hosted a memoria dedication honoring the true heroes of 9/11.

A heart warming, patriotic and emotional CD commemorating that memorable day has been produced. Randy Deaver and Crossfire per formed a one-hour show to over 1,000 Central California firefighters, law enforcement personnel and valley fans. Rick Babenik, Executive Pro ducer and Owner of Rixana Records, dedicated the CD to all California's public servants who put their lives on the line every day. Dan Johnson performed his unforgettable song titled "The Bravest" to a tearful audi ence as two new videos from the CD debuted in the background. Over ,233 CD's were sold. Partial proceeds go directly to the FDNY UFA JFOA and NYPD PBA Widow's and Children's Fund. The CD is titled California: A Memorial Tribute to 9/11/01).

Days following the Dec. 8th memorial, several e-mails from New York and Calif. Firefighters & Policemen were received requesting their songs Dozen of telephone calls from radio stations throughout the country have

requested a copy. In fact, it s just now beginning to receive regular airplay on many stations and because Los Angeles also sent several hundred firefighters to New York, the duo has been approached about the CD as a fund raiser for the LAFD and a request for them to perform at severa LA firehouses.

California: A Memorial Tribute to 9/11 consist of 5 selections. It begins with an emotional and powerful ar rangement of "The Pledge of Alle giance" produced and arranged by award winning producer Jeff Hall of Maximus Media in Fresno followed by the NYPD Emerald Pipes & Drums version of "Amazing Grace". The third selection is the most memo rable, "The Bravest" written by Tom Paxton and performed by Dan Johnson, followed by a live and highly charged version of Lee Greenwood's "God Bless the USA" performed by Randy Deaver. The final cut is a simple song titled "People that Matter". It is a song about the everyday people in our lives that go the extra mile to help a stranger. The song was first released on his debut CD titled "Senses".

This CD is available for sale on the CSFA website. Go to www.csfa.net for more information.

An Interview with Michael Megna:

"After the 9/11 attacks, we worked on renovating the buildings. Our captain, Anthony Whitaker, was worried about his men and felt a need to get morale up. On this particular day, Captain Whitaker needed a locksmith, so I went with him through the Holland Tunnel to headquarters. When we got there, I saw the *Pelco Press* on the technician's bench. I wondered how it got there, where it came from. I looked through it as we traveled back through the Holland Tunnel.

"Later, I called Pelco to receive some memorial books and was put through to Diana. She asked what I was going to use them for, as she wanted to share that information with Mr. McDonald. She sent me twelve books.

"I noticed that a plaque that had been made for the fallen had "New York's Finest" and "New York's Bravest" and "Flight 93" mentioned on it, but not the Port Authority. Port Authority are not city police. The World Trade Center was a Port Authority facility. Mayor Giuliani kept referring to his police and his fire fighters – but no mention of the Port Authority though the Port Authority Executive Director and thirty-six others had died in the attack. There was no one to speak up for them and let people know about the Port Authority but they had done most of the evacuation.

"The first week of November, Diana called from Pelco and invited me to attend the memorial they were having. I said that I would like to bring Captain Whitaker with me. Tony and I were not sure whether we could get away to attend the memorial, so I asked Diana if Mr. McDonald would call my superiors to request that we attend. After 9/11, Port Authority officers were ordered to work six to seven days a week, twelve hours a day, no vacations allowed. Mr. McDonald called and spoke to the chief. Tony received a call from the chief telling him that both he and I should definitely attend. We acted like we didn't know anything about it and accepted.

"A few months after the memorial, Pelco and the New York Police, Fire Department, and Port Authority planned a 2002 St. Patrick's Day reunion. I helped secure the pier where the party was held. I also organized the tour buses to the WTC and Ground Zero for that time. In June of 2003, our work hours were reduced back to eight-hour work tours. In July of that year I had a heart attack and was out sick for nearly a year. I retired in March of 2004."

Michael Megna
Port Authority of NY & NJ Retired

THE GENERAL CHUCK YEAGER FOUNDATION

General Chuck Yeager Foundation
PO Box 579
Penn Valley, CA. 95946
www.chuckyeager.com

The General Chuck Yeager Foundation has endowment funds for scholarships at Women in Aviation International, Marshall University's Yeager Scholars, a four year scholarship that includes a semester abroad and a summer course at Oxford University and EAA's young Eagles Air Academy. General Yeager flies Young Eagles and Make-A-Wish Foundation children. He participates in fund raisers for those with Down Syndrome and Autism. He raises funds for disabled and paralyzed veterans.